Barbadian Popular Music and the Politics of Caribbean Culture

BARBADIAN POPULAR MUSIC AND THE POLITICS OF CARIBBEAN CULTURE

Curwen Best

Schenkman Books, Inc.
Rochester • Vermont

Copyright ©1999

Schenkman Books, Inc.
118 Main Street
Rochester, Vermont 05767 USA

http://www.sover.net/~schenkma/
e-mail: schenkma@sover.net

Library of Congress Cataloging-in-Publication Data

Best, Curwen, 1965-

    Barbadian popular music and the politics of Caribbean culture/by
Curwen Best.
    p. cm.
    Originally published: Farmingdale, New York: AC Inc., ©1995.
    Discography:
    Includes bibliographical references (p.) and index.
    ISBN 0-87047-111-2 (pbk.)
    1. Popular music—Barbados—History and criticism. 2. Political ballads
and songs—Barbados—History and criticism. 3. Politics and culture-—
Caribbean Area. 4. Music and society—Caribbean Area.
    I. Title.
    ML3486.B35B47 1998
    781.63'0972981--dc21
    97-50597
    CIP
    MN

Printed in the United States of America

ACKNOWLEDGMENTS

To:
God for the strength and ability • Schenkman Books for believing in this work • Bajan artists, musicians and all involved in the industry • Grant Music Ltd. • ICE Records for permission to reproduce most of the lyrics in this book

Mr. Eddy Grant for his time, insight, endorsement and insistence that I go through with this pioneering book. He has exhibited as much enthusiasm for this project as he has shown towards Caribbean and Barbadian music over the years.

Especially to:
Anthony Nicholas Carter, known as Gabby, Barbados' greatest music legend • ICE Record's Ms. Dawn C. Gill-Thomas • Rainbow Wirl's Ms. Kay McConney and Wirl's stockroom posse • Trever Marshall the true pioneer in this field • Wayne "Poonka" Willock • Adisa Andwele • Peter Ram • Mark Williams • Lil' Man • Shane Boodhoo and Sounds Gud • Project Band Massive Sound • Carl Wade • Mike Alleyne • Ruth Archer • Fay Brandon • Andrea King • Jacqueline Cummins • A. Brian Gooding • Carl Kellman

I feel I have left out so many names of other individuals who have contributed in one way or another—I hope you will forgive me.

Thanks to you all.

Most of all,
thanks to my family
who have been my
greatest God-given inspiration.

And to Charmaine.

Curwen Best

PUBLISHING CREDIT

All songs credited to Gabby
were written and composed by Anthony Carter
and published by Grant Music Ltd.

All songs credited to Viking Tundah
were written by Shirland Bowen
and published by ICE Music Ltd.

All songs credited to Sparrow
were written and composed by Slinger Francisco
and published by ICE Music Ltd.

FOREWORD

The facts and the truth, as they relate to history, can be diametrically opposed one to the other, especially in relation to matters of culture wherein egos and personal agendas may cause writers to glorify or under glorify events as they transpire.

In speaking at some length with Dr. Curwen Best, I got the impression that here was a young man intent upon establishing the truth with regard to one aspect of culture in Barbados.

To my knowledge, there has never been a book such as this on the music to be found in Barbados, and because there is such a dearth of good books on Caribbean music I would hope that some time in the future Dr. Best would consider extending his dissertation on music to the rest of the region.

Maybe I should choose this time to make a few observations about facts that are not generally known in or around Caribbean music circles, but, like "Columbus discovered the West Indies," have been used to damaging effect in our culture by those who should know better and those literary parasites who only regurgitate what they can find in the supposed researched writings of others, and which then enter into the pantheon of "fact."

For example: It has been chronicled to death that reggay (now "reggae" finally) has its genesis rooted and routed in early American dance music. In particular it is touted that it was the music of New Orleans—which Jamaicans are supposed to have heard in the 1950s from Miami radio stations—that gave ska/ bluebeat its sound and swing.

Everybody seems kind of happy with this, while forgetting the very nature of Caribbean people; in particular the musicians of the other islands who have a particular penchant for altering the swing of the music of their sister isles.

According to the great calypsonian Roaring Lion, this has happened with very serious effect in Trinidad and Tobago, wherein many of the original calypsos which are claimed as having been written by Trinidadians, were in fact brought to Trinidad by either sailors or artists from other islands, or just itinerant travellers (i.e., the song now known as "Mathilda").

In the history of Jamaican music two names come readily to mind, those of the great Barbadian singer and musician Jackie Opel and Trinidadian guitarist and arranger Nerlin Taitt, sometimes referred to as Lyn Taitt.

I know for certain that even if Jamaicans are aware of the contribution these stalwarts have made to their national musics, for sure it would be hard to find among their own countrymen and women ones who recognize the sterling work done by these brothers, in trying to bring about true musical Caribbean unity.

Over the last sixteen years I've witnessed Gabby trying to convince Barbadians of the magnitude of Jackie Opel's contribution to the Jamaican and Barbadian musical landscape.

A few years ago, at my insistence, Nerlin Taitt was finally honored by the people of his region of Trinidad and Tobago but although he was recognized in his region as an ace steelpan arranger while living in Trinidad, his contribution to the evolution of reggae is still to be nationally and regionally recognized.

Some years ago amid a raging media argument about my "hard to dispute" claim to having conceptualized soca (I called it kaisoul, as in kaiso or calypso and soul) the famous Jamaican artist, DJ and TV presenter Mikey Dread and I were discussing some of the things I have done in music. I mentioned to him that people have great difficulty in believing the degree to which I have been involved in all genres of music and in fact pointed out to him that I had also written, performed and produced two of the great reggae (well, ska/rock steady) standards and they were "Train Tour to Rainbow City" and "Rough Rider." Mikey, like everyone else, thought these to be Prince Buster songs as Buster had covered them but they had been successful long before Buster did them. He called his cover version "Train to Girls Town."

As a matter of fact, "Train Tour to Rainbow City" was the first British-produced ska recording to make the national chart in England (#31 in the top 50).

One day while discussing Caribbean music with the great Jamaican producer and reggae historian Bunny Lee, he happened to mention to me the impact of the first kaisoul/soka/soca recording on Jamaican society.

He said "bwoy Aggro"—he calls me and I call him Aggro, hence the name of his studio band The Aggravators—

> ...you nuh really know how da tune mash up Jamaica. Dem seh ah de only Pap-tune weh rastaman binna dance to dem time deh, caas bwoy, dem time deh rastaman binna serious man inna Jamaica. Hear me man, dat saang was suh serious dat dem use to call P.J. Patterson [currently Prime Minister of Jamaica] 'Black Skin Blue Eyed Bwoy' when him was younger. Some a dem still ah call 'im suh.

This would have been late 1970 or early 1971 and onward in the Caribbean including—you guessed it—Trinidad and Tobago.

It seems to me that certainly in the Caribbean we tend to want to nationalize and then insularize music very much as we do our countries, or we want other people to play "our music" upon "our terms"—remember that we don't really create, we only conceptualize music in a different shape.

Soca was conceptualized to bring calypso closer to a more universal Afro-Caribbean dance music with lyrics that could be easily understood the world over. It was indiginized and insularized and retrograded into becoming a new form of calypso. So much so was this done that at one time the DJs and the all-knowing experts tried to give the accolade to Lord Kitchener, Maestro, Shadow and then finally Lord Shorty. At least Sparrow came out and said he is not a soca man; Maestro died before any embarrassment could be attached to him; and Kitchener, the gentleman that he is, did not commit himself fully in any direction, leaving the rest to find the truth.

Lord Shorty actually met me at the Belvedere Hotel (Guyana) in the 1970s and congratulated me on "changing the music of Trinidad and Tobago" as he felt "calypso is dead." Why then did he accept the mantle and allow a good concept to go the wrong way?

Now here we are at the frontier of a new millennium and after being challenged by some friends who have said that the only way the doubters would stop doubting my claim to the above mentioned facts would be for me to "create" another concept.

On that day, in my sound engineer Frank Aggarat's backyard I told them that within five years I would have established a whole new concept, which would be for the first time in our cultural history, a youth-oriented life-style to include a totally original work, sound and stated philosophy. That concept is called *ringbang*, you know it, you now dance to it exclusively if you are young and expressive enough. For the first time in our history a music has been established solely for youth and there's a veritable plethora of young artists from Jamaica to Guyana playing ringbang music. You know what else is also happening? History is repeating itself. This time Barbados is trying to claim ringbang and for now, certainly in this transitory period, people are still saying soca when they are playing or talking about ringbang.

Finally there is now a beautiful color magazine released quarterly which is dedicated to the ringbang life-style, and it is called, you guessed it, *Ringbang*. And as I write this Foreword, the Caribbean News Association (CANA) radio network has entered into an agreement with that magazine to present a radio program based solely on the content and style of the magazine, and that program will be called Ringbang.

As we enter the new millennium, Caribbean music has changed and we must all accept that change for the survival of a truly Caribbean culture. That culture will be proliferated around the universe by our youth. If this book by Dr. Curwen Best helps to demarcate our cultural progress sufficient for the reader to appreciate us as a Caribbean people a little more, he will have set the stage for maybe a greater demand on our young writers to show further sides of us to the world.

Good luck, Dr. Best.

Eddy Grant
April 21, 1998

CONTENTS

PART ONE

Introduction 1
1   Discursive Centers 5
Theories, Implications and Applications
Tuk History, Theory and Aesthetics
2   Cultural Interactivity and Caribbean Criticism 24
Literary Into Cultural Studies
Calypso Judging Performance

PART TWO

3   Music and Culture in the Twentieth Century 43
A Precursor: Before 1960
Why Spouge "Died"
4   Centering an Artist 58
Gabby and the Entertainment Industry: 1950-1970
Folk Music and Contemporary Society
5   The Commercial Edge: Soca and After 83
Kai-Soca and Politics
Ringbang as Cultural Appropriation?
6   Popular Bands, Gospel and Dub Culture 119
Popular Bands: Technology and the Industry
Denominational Politics in the Name of the Gospel
Dancehall and Dub
7   Conclusion 140
Glossary 150
Selected Discography of Barbadian Music 155
Bibliography 161

INTRODUCTION

The purpose of this book is to document, analyze and theorize on the music of Barbados and Barbadian culture. Since there is no other text that I know of which is seriously devoted to the music of Barbados, this book goes about the task of creating a context for the conceptualization and analysis of Barbadian music forms such as tuk and spouge, as well as other rhythms performed on the island. There have been a number of books on the music of other Caribbean territories, but until now there has been no definitive text on the music of Barbados.

In as much as the music entertainment industry in Barbados has expanded within the 1980s, this development has not been accompanied by supporting critical documentation, appraisal, analysis, contextualization and academic legitimization. This book does not set out to document the complete detailed history of music in Barbados, but it can be said that it deals with the major aspects of music and musical performance on this island, stretching from the seventeenth century to the present day. Readers of this book will remark that its treatment of the music and culture of Barbados is informed by a theoretical awareness (but one which is not obtrusive).

The first two chapters are concerned with relating the music forms of Barbados to broader spheres of understanding. For example, the section on tuk theory provides a history of Barbados' first indigenous music form as well as provides a framework for applying tuk's historical, socio-political, cultural and musical significance to other works of art and genres. Chapter Two takes up this suggestion of musical-literary interactivity and demonstrates the relationship between the music of the Caribbean and its literature. Chapter Three is less theoretical and more direct in dealing with music and culture in Barbados. I should also make special mention of the section in Chapter Three which centers on spouge in the 1970s. This section stands out partly because it seeks to refute a popular conception that spouge's demise came about because of an inherent musical monotony. This section is also important because it makes the point that the post-1970s expansion of the music entertainment industry in Barbados was built largely on the prior achievements and developments of the 1970s spouge era.

Chapters Four and Five take up the artist Anthony "Gabby" Carter as their major focus, concentrating on his work within the genres of folk, calypso, soca and ringbang. They explore the dynamics of Barbadian music from the 1960s through the 1990s. Chapter Six is even more up-to-date and incisive in its analysis of important aspects to Barbadian music and culture such as gospel, pop bands, technology, dub, the media and the interface with the international industry. It is concerned with the politics which influence and inform the national culture.

This book is intended for a general readership; for those who have an interest in Caribbean music and culture. It should prove to be a very important text for students and teachers at all levels of the educational system, and across a number of subject areas and disciplines. It documents and validates a culture and its practices which have, up to now, had to depend on the authority of public discussion to assert their legitimacy. This book will also be of interest to academics with an interest in cultural studies, popular music and culture, and theory of culture and literature.

PART ONE

1 DISCURSIVE CENTERS

THEORIES, IMPLICATIONS AND APPLICATION

Concomitant with the growing interest in orature in African and non-Western cultures was an equally fervent interest in the tools of examining, analyzing and expounding on the works in this field. Therefore, the first recourse for explorers into the verbal arts of these cultures was to revert to the twentieth century fathers of oral theory, Milman Parry and Albert Lord. First introduced by Parry in 1930 in "The Studies in the Epic Techniques of Oral Verse Making, I: Homer and Homeric Style"[1] and later buttressed by Lord in the long revered The Singer of Tales,[2] was their formulaic theory. Parry had sought to differentiate between the method of composition for the oral and scribal poet. This led to the concept that the oral artist, always under pressure to compose, often reverts to ". . . a group of words which is regularly employed under the same metric conditions to express a given essential idea."[3]

The major thrust of their formulaic theory (which has undergone much criticism and many adaptations) must be the onus which it places on the composition process as the major distinction between oral and scribal forms. What the years subsequent to their conclusions have steadily revealed is the limited and limiting usefulness of their theory. As far afield as Russia, Patricia Arant was applying the theory to a form of Russian oral poetry (Bylina). Though seeing clusters of formula that were correlated, she noted that there were improvisational performers who neither created nor produced a fixed formulaic pattern.[4] Larry

Benson, in his essay "The Literary Character of Anglo-Saxon Formulaic Theory," later postulated that any writer could successfully imitate the formulaic style.[5]

Within the African sphere specifically, Ruth Finnegan does not become overly preoccupied with the formulaic emphasis on performance and composition as a theoretical guide to the study of orature. Neither does she privilege the structural approach of Levi-Strauss and his followers.[6] She places greater emphasis on the actual performance and on questions of setting, situation, audience, audience/performer interplay, performer style, expression and improvisation. Most other commentators on orature (in the African context) are preoccupied with the peculiarities of the geographical, cultural and linguistic boundaries. Hence, current research sets out to examine individual traditional modes rather than to establish any broad theoretical generalizations. Arguably, this is the most appropriate procedure for a cultural area as diverse as Africa and the Diaspora, and for a region like the Caribbean in particular.

Kofi Anyidoho takes the onus away from composition as the main basis of the distinction between written, oral and sung literature. He contends:

> . . . the distinction lies, not in the process of composition, but in the mode of realization for what is composed. For the oral poet as well as for the scribal poet the composition and its realization may sometimes but not always be co-temporal. Composition, however will always be mental . . .[7]

While the focus on distinctive traditions has gained momentum and acceptance, there is still the lingering question of the needed and preferred theoretical, disciplinary or methodological approach for engaging with the oral and music arts. Ime Ikiddeh, in referring to the interdisciplinary nature of oral literature, cautions that:

> Criticism of oral literature must be ready when the need arises to make use of anthropological data, the material of oral history the wealth of socio-linguistics, and the notations of traditional musical forms without turning its essence into those pursuits.[8]

It was to such a question of approach that the 1989 Discourse and Disguises Conference at the Center of West African Studies, University of Birmingham (UK), sought to address. By collating the many disciplinary standpoints in interpreting oral texts, it proposed to move forward towards greater interdisciplinary interaction. This premise was agreed to be the desirable method, though its difficulty was acknowledged. Karin Barber went even further by calling for more than collaboration between experts from several disciplines, "Rather than collaboration between specialists from different disciplines, what is needed is the reintegration of an artificially divided field."[9] True, her suggestion restates a method which has been postulated before (as the previous quotation attests), but this restatement emanates from a perception that such an orientation has hardly been attempted with any consistency of purpose.

In her 1992 text on oral traditions and research practices, Ruth Finnegan gives a very clear overview of the various influential methodological and theoretical approaches to the study of oral arts and verbal traditions. Beginning with nineteenth and early twentieth century theories, she refers to origin, development, deterioration and myth-ritual theories, as well as the Finnish historical-geographic method.[10] Among the more contemporary approaches are those based on Marxist, post-Structuralist, performance-centered, discourse and feminist perspectives. Each of these perspectives is not totally exclusive of the others. In fact, what is quite common to most of these more contemporary outlooks is their challenge to established notions surrounding the creation, production, function, structure, context, study and interpretation of the work of art. Marxist perspectives are often driven by politics wherein:

> The process of social and cultural reproduction are seen as essentially bound in with current social conditions . . . unlike the a-social framework of many historical-geographical or psychological approaches.[11]

In order to counter previous gender biases in classification and presentation of the oral arts, some feminist perspectives emphasize the need to be sensitive to the role of gender, the female's identity and voice, and the woman's social position and actions.[12] Post-Structuralist themes, such as multiple rather than single meanings and its general questioning of fixed models of text and meaning, have come into the domain of recent studies of verbal arts. Most performance-centered approaches view audience participation as vital constituents of the performance:

> The totally passive audience is a figment of the imagination.... Performance is about . . . a continuous negotiation between stage and auditorium to establish the significance of the signs and conventions through which they interact.[13]

Modern discourse-centered analyses are usually sensitive to the paralinguistic, musical and kinetic aspects of performance and they challenge other limitations to only literary forms.[14]

Again, there can be much overlap between these theoretical positions. In referring to their usefulness to oral discourse, Finnegan is of the firm belief that ". . . they are seldom totally divided in practice and some of the best studies draw on a mixture."[15] She places such current and future trends of approach under the heading of Pluralism. For her, such interdisciplinary approaches do not represent ad hoc kinds of inquiry. Such studies are concerned with the interaction of oral and written forms, emergent Creole forms, ethnographically specific fields, performer-audience dynamics and flexibility of text.[16] She emphasizes the importance of building on some of the relevant older work as a foundation for future studies and development. She concludes with the caution, "In the last analysis the approaches are only as good—and as separate—as the uses made of them."[17]

This study of Barbadian music does not begin with any single theoretical imperative. Its greater focus is on documenting and analyzing movements in the development of Barbadian music and culture. This book also pays attention to the relationship between music and other Barbadian artistic genres and phenomena. Cross-references are made to other art forms and disciplines. This method represents my perception of the importance of making a connection between the wide range of art forms within the Caribbean.

TUK HISTORY, THEORY AND AESTHETICS

From as early as 1660 there was a set of slave laws in place which saw to the governing of "Negroes" in Barbados and sought to curtail overt manifestations of artistic practices. It was with subsequent amendments and specifications that the 1688 code threateningly warned the African not to "beat drums, blow horns, or use loud instruments."[18] Although there would be a rabid preoccupation with this type of censorship,[19] William Dickson, a British citizen residing in Barbados around 1788, alluding to the drum being prohibited, makes specific reference to:

> The black musicians [who], however, have substituted in its place, a common earthen jar, on beating the aperture of which, with the extended palms of their hands, it emits a hollow sound, resembling the more animating note of the drum.[20]

Handler and Frisbie[21] attest to this integral function of music in slave society as does the J.W. Orderson novel *Creoleana*.[22] In addition, the 1971-1973 pioneering archaeological research project in Barbados led Handler and Lange to surmise that:

> Houses also probably contained, albeit with less frequency, other items which slaves are known to have used or manufactured: such items could have included various types of baskets, fishnets . . . and musical devices like drums, rattles and stringed instruments.[23]

A survey of the sketches, letters and travelogues on early Barbadian practices and lifestyle (though the documents are far from being reliable historical sources) provides enough evidence to confirm the existence of what must have been active and functioning bands.[24] For example, George Pinckard's writing on African-Barbadian slave practices reports:

> The instrumental parts of the band consist of a species of drum, a kind of rattle, and the ever-delightful banjar. The first is a long hollow piece of wood, with a dried sheep-skin tied over the end, the second is a calabash containing a number of small stones fixed to a short stick which serves as the handle . . .[25]

These predominantly percussive bands, usually of about four members, who would come together to play on special occasions, might supplement their makeup by an additional number on great occasions. These occasions include the symbolic "crop over" celebrations that mark the end of the reaping of the sugarcane plant or some other festive occasion such as the Christmas holiday gatherings.[26] In *Notes for a Glossary of Words and Phrases of Barbadian Dialect*,[27] Frank Collymore offers a gloss for *took* (noun) as "crude musical sounds; to play took and banjo." The Bajan phenomenon of tuk band music dates back to the days when the slaves arrived. The band and its music symbolize the continuation of African musical expression in the "New World." Although the early data on performance techniques and actual musical makeup of the rhythms were ethnocentric and subjectively descriptive, the mere fact that it was heard as something unlike anything the European was familiar with must give some credence to the assumptions that here might have been the beginnings of what is by far the more significant of the two indigenous rhythms of Barbados.[28] To Pinckard, the rhythms of the slaves' music added up to "noisy sounds" which required "only a slight aid from fancy to transport [the listener] to the savage wilds of Africa."[29]

Furthermore, where the ethnographic data refers to the proclivity towards polyrhythms, call and response type rhythmic structures, variations of tempo, and intricate patterning, there is a marked connection between what was and what is now known as the phenomenon of tuk.[30]

It is the African-derived sense of performance, with its supposed accent or emphasis on rhythm, which is responsible and accounts for the ideophonic name given to this phenomenon: *tuk*. In "Interpretation in a West Indian Language Situation," Peter Roberts observes how, "The ideophone is somewhat more developed [than the onomatopoeia] in that on its own it can give a lot of information without supplementary words."[31]

Arguably, the lexical item tuk derives informally from a shortened version of ruk-a-tuk music, itself an ideophonic sound-image of the music of the band, and especially of the snare drum's rapid and sharply resonating rolls. Tuk may also have originated from Bumbatuk, the first two syllables echoing the bounce and resonance (alternating tonal textures created by damping and release) produced by, at and on the bass drum, the central time-piece of this band.

After Emancipation a major stimulus for the enhancement and development of the tuk band came with the inauguration of a friendly society called the Landship. In addition to the philan-thropic and charitable practice of distributing possessions and rotating funds, the Landship also came together to engage in public masquerades of marine activity—imitating, building upon and exaggerating the movements of the ship at sea and of its sailors at work.[32] The tuk band became an integral component and affiliate of the Landship movement. The tuk band provided the rhythms of the sea—slow, medium or fast—mirroring the states of the ocean and creating a more visibly and audibly intriguing spectacle for the patrons to whom the Landship performed. The tuk rhythms gave a fuller form and expression to the mimetic antics of the Landship's sailors, creating greater interaction between performers and audiences, who surrendered themselves to and swayed with the repeated infectious beatings of the tuk band. This performance is carried over into contempo-rary Barbadian society. It is common to see the observer getting into the rhythm and vicariously submerging him or herself within the performance antics of the Landship's crew. It is when the ship is at full steam with "160 pounds of pressure" (presumably referring to the amount of pressure which was required to propel the actual steam boat at full speed) that rhythmic improvisation and the expressiveness of dance take over. Then there is an unconscious proximity to the state of possession which is associ-ated with Shango, Voodoo, Pocomania, Zion and Baptist rituals in other Caribbean contexts. Wayne "Poonka" Willock, a lead-ing tuk player, remarks that "it [the tuk band] is the engine of the boat [Landship]."[33] This bears some connection to Edward Kamau Brathwaite's concept of African survivals in worship and to Shango (the god who possesses the locomotive in the New World). But this state of possession associated with the tuk band and the Landship is a distinctively Afro-Bajan phenomenon.

Since the Landship depended on financial and other types of generosity for its functioning, its alliance with the tuk band would be long-lasting. Together they could generate much excitement and response from their patrons. Both the tuk band and the Landship exemplify the level of creativity and distortion which the Afro-Bajan would bear on imposed notions of some European "standard" (i.e., instrument, music, etc.), or in other words, the Landship movement is a conscious subversion of the activities and antics of British sailors and their vessels at sea. The physical movements of the Landship thus became a medium through which they were able to perpetuate the rhythms and dances of Africa. Their antics have also been embellished to attract audiences and to acquire rewards to buttress their financial associations. Similarly, the tuk band has used European instruments but inscribed its own African-derived sense of rhythm and orchestration.

The contemporary tuk band is made up of the bass drum, snare or kettle drum, penny-whistle or flute, and a percussive ideophonic instrument, usually a triangle, although "this can be augmented at times with a second kettle drum as well as several other percussion instruments . . ."[34] Such a bland listing of instruments involved does not do justice to the kind of interpretation, vibrancy, spontaneity, flexibility and transformations which the tuk exponents bring to the playing and treatment of these instruments.

The versatility of the tuk band is evidenced in its wide repertoire of songs. It is not novel to hear the band perform Euro-classical pieces, Negro spirituals, or selected popular Billboard tracks.[35] But it is through the performance of indigenous and Caribbean songs that the musicians appear most comfortable and their impact on audiences is most striking. At such moments, the interaction between man and instrument, instrument and instrument, and performer and audience can take over. This leads to many deliberate, intriguing transgressions against notions of formulaic procedure. Consequently, such preconceptions of what is the "original" meter, accent, rhythm and general orchestration become the servants of improvisation as the audience taunts and inspires and the penny-whistle player leads his orchestra into a display of musical and dramatic explorations. The tuk band is said to have patterned itself on the marching band of eighteenth-century British military regiments.[36] Arguably, many of the Afro-Bajan musicians must have been intrigued by the British military regiments, particularly of the fact that the British bandsmen all carried their instruments. But the British bands did not interpret its musical texts with lavish, skillful, aesthetically brilliant and suggestive body movements, or with the kinds of vocal "hollas" and shouts which have become trademarks of the tuk band tradition.

In the mid-1970s and especially with the advent of Barbados' Crop Over Festival as a government policy-induced celebration, there has been a growing tolerance of the tuk band by the Establishment. There is still, however, an ignorance concerning the socio-historical and cultural purpose and function of the tuk band as an indigenous entity. For the "folk" and majority of Bajans over thirty years old, the tuk band has served as a medium of entertainment, an occasion for social interaction, and as a symbol of Bajan indigenous creativity. Recently, the tuk band has increasingly been projected as a tourist product. Its growing absence from the activities of the local communities connotes a loss of the band's spontaneity and its performers real sense of interaction with their society. The staging of formal tuk band competitions is one example of policy attempts at the institutionalization of a phenomenon which already should have been seen as an institution sui generis.

Before the aforementioned period but within the twentieth century, the tuk band and its music were integral parts of both secular and religious festivities. On bank holidays (public holidays) it was not uncommon to see this roving band of practitioners encroaching on, overtaking and inviting themselves into the domains of popular gatherings (i.e., picnics, outings, etc.). There they would do a series of impromptu or rehearsed numbers all to the favor of the onlookers. Appreciative audiences might reward them with money, but more often with food or something to drink. Willock adds:

> . . . traditionally tuk band will come out and play and . . . before it used to carry a stigma or what we would call a taboo where most of the fellas were old, they were into alcohol, they would play for rum

... it was a community thing, because of dis stigma you find it was like a rum shop ting so if de fellas came out and play, you would find, well, some people give them a shot o' rum or something.[37]

Foreday Christmas Morning (early dawn)[38] was the preferred time of all other religious festivals when this band, along with cantors, would serenade from outside the windows of many a house, in hopes of receiving payment. Poonka records and recreates such an event in his 1983 calypso "Tuk Band Rhythm:"

Icky-do Icky-do here I stand
Open de windows listen to de band
For my band sweet as honey
Open de window throw de money
Listen to de music that I bring
Ah bottle of rum is just de ting
Little Jesus meek and mild
Two rum for a man and one for a child.[39]

In this type of practice one observed the fusing of what in the strictest (Western) sense might be termed as religious and secular tradition. However, for the tuk band players, this festival was another way they would shape and re-shape their craft in order to suit the occasion and to be effective in evoking some response from their audience. Thus, the chant might differ on another occasion and be replaced by another recitation. As with some of their forerunners in the West African context, Barbadian roving performers are noted for covering themes as diverse as death and marriage.

The tuk men would go to all lengths of their imaginative know-how in order to affect their aims. During my research among the elderly I found anecdotes of a number of interesting encounters between the tuk band and its patrons. Among them was one of a house-dweller's reluctance to open his door to the tuk man's pleas early one Christmas morning. When the tuk man notices a beautiful garden all arrayed and prepared for the ostentatious "showin' off" in Christmas daylight, he sings out with an exaggerated march:

Uh mashing down yuh garden
Uh mashing down yuh garden
Uh mashing down yuh garden
Uh mashing down yuh garden[40]

The window was opened in haste, only to find the garden still untouched and the tuk musicians laughing in triumph that they have yet again been able to entertain and induce. Then the cantor or whistle player starts off and the whole band performs for their due. The events of this occurrence are similar to the audience-performer awareness which Egudu and Nwoga constantly refer to in the Igbo context. They speak of the audience being "taken out of themselves" and "immersed in the mood of the song."

Within the contemporary tuk band the bass drum is basically similar to the type employed by regimental and other marching bands. It is worn or carried by the musician, appended to a strap which sits diagonally across his shoulder, the drum's center extending no lower or higher than the hips. The difference in technique between this tuk drummer and the player within the militia is that the tuk man uses only one mallet. He employs the other hand (usually the least flexible one) for creating tonal contrasts through damping on the drum's skin. For one tuk player, the bass drum "carries the swing of the band."[41] By this one assumes that he refers to its metrical function as the band's most central time-piece. What one hears from a tuk band in full performance is a collage of rhythmic punctuation, contrasts, embellishments, counterpoint and cross or polyrhythms. Within the composition of real tuk—that is, tuk in its up-tempo 4/4 variety—the bass drummer might frequently (appear to) punctuate the first beat of each bar and subsequently dampen the duration of a half beat; or he might alternate this pattern by playing and then damping for the same duration as above—a beat and a half—but now, beginning on the second beat and punctuating the fourth beat of each bar as well. I should stress that this interpretation of the bass drum's pattern is not fixed. It only refers to what might occasionally be heard as its orchestral resultant. Listening to the sample of up-tempo numbers by Ruk-A-Tuk International on *Indigenous Tuk Band Music of Barbados* reconfirms this perception. However, there is no such thing as a formula for what a bass drum player should or should not play. It is especially in live performances that he punctuates all four beats in a common time number, though on these occasions one has to employ both ear and eye to record what the bass drum is actual phrasing. The point with which I am laboring here is that when someone moves or dances to tuk (or observes others dancing), it is a movement which responds to much more than the bass drum's phrasing. The dance is often more vibrant than a sole reliance on the bass drum's rhythm might produce. This is not to say that the bass drum does not contribute to the whole textural makeup of the band's sound. The point is that the tuk band's music is characterized by numerous rhythms and cross rhythms which makes it perilous to attribute its transmitted rhythmic response to any one instrument.

The snare or kettle drum is worn in a similar fashion to the bass drum. Its player uses two standard size sticks with which he executes rapid, improvised rolls through flexible movements of the wrist. This drum is basically the same as the snare in a standard five-piece set. Although it is called the snare or kettle drum, it is really "snare-less." This instrument is perhaps the most rhythmically active and dynamic of all those which comprise the tuk band. Within its 4/4 time interpretations, the snare player often interprets in rolls of 1/16 and 1/32 parts of a beat. The snare often sounds in contrast to the bass drum. Most noticeable is its sharper, less resonant texture of sound which is weighed against the deeper bass drum, even when the bass drum plays its staccato phrases (executed by damping). It is this contrast which creates much of the tonal, rhythmic and textural interest within the band.

Tuk is characterized by the almost consistent rising and falling of tonal properties after the bass drum's entry gives way to the snare's sharper tone and usually shorter intervals. To speak of the relationship between the snare and the brass drums within the band so stagnantly, stringently, distinctly and logically as I have done here distorts the reality of the kinds of rapid, indistinguishable, indiscriminate processes and relationships which go on, characterizing real tuk in its actual performance context. It is important to note that the structuring noted above can and often does occur when the tuk band is in full swing; its musicians interpreting their parts within metrical phrases whose tempo is often in excess of 130 beats per minute.

The penny-whistle is approximately the same size as the piccolo. It is pitched an octave above the Euro-classical flute, its compass spanning from an octave above middle C and upwards approximately a whole octave. It is held straight up and down when played. Unlike related aerophones, it is played with six fingers as opposed to eight. It was often made from the wild bamboo which proliferated the sideways and shrubby patches of vegetation throughout the island. Since the 1950s the penny-whistle has taken an even more integral role within the band, being used with increasing frequency and instead of the solo cantor. Since it is the only instrument in the band which is capable of wide-ranging melodic properties, it carries the melodic line. It often starts off each song, occasionally interpreting two to four bars unaccompanied before the total ensemble joins in. This has the function of helping to clearly define what is going on; of indicating what song is being played. Such a function does not denote that this instrument cannot improvise, since after the melodic line is clearly defined some levels of free variation are possible. But the penny-whistle inevitably reverts to, or as clearly as possible approximates, the formulaic outline of a prescribed melodic text.

The steel, or triangle, is the final basic component of the band's makeup. Its sound and place, though vital to the compositional texture and the sum output timbre of any tuk band, does not command a central position within the band's contemporary manifestation. On a few occasions the steel is enhanced by the use of some other membrane-vibrating ideophone such as the maracas or cow bell. Its function is, for the most part, embellishing and maintaining a series of fixed repetitive patterns when the patterns are felt out and taken up. The steel is held at its apex with one hand and beaten with a slender metal implement held in the other.

There are similar types of bands within the region with closely related rhythms, such as the "mumming bands" of St. Kitts, Nevis and Jamaica. The players' similarity in African background and tradition account for much of this shared influence. However, there are marked distinctions not only in terms of the composition of the Barbadian tuk band and its sister and brother institutions within the Caribbean cultural region, but also in terms of the songs played, the bands' sound, and some rhythmic peculiarities and distinctions. The tuk band, by name and rhythm, is native and indigenous to Barbados.

Within the Caribbean area, Brathwaite has put forth a number of intriguing insights (though too abstract and extra-disciplinary for serious pursuit) for conceiving the similarity between the structure of some Caribbean novels and African-American jazz. Admittedly, his insights require expansion and further application as a prelude to the formulation of theory.

Others have also seen and heard a similarity between the music of the region and its other cultural and artistic genres. There has been talk of Selvon's technical and stylistic proximity to the language of calypso (but serious development and theory appears sketchy and parenthetical at best).[42] In spite of the different modes and media of manifestation of the arts in the region, they are unmistakably connected. Music, dance, drama, verse and literature are interrelated within the perception of a Caribbean aesthetics.

However, at the level of propounding a theory or general framework for an holistic approach to or perception and interpretation of the formal literary text based on the composition and structures of an oral medium, Brathwaite's approach comes closest. It would be intriguing, as well as theoretically and aesthetically groundbreaking, if some of the formal works of literature from the region could be creatively interpreted, read and heard through the reconstructed structures of indigenous Caribbean cultural forms. Where, for instance, the composition or makeup of the steel band and its designated parts might form the analogical or symbolic framework from which insights into a collected body of oral and written texts, or into an artist's, performer's or writer's craft, might be perceived, expounded and shared. One might, for instance, take the tenor steel pans, double second, guitar, cello pans and bass and relate their orchestral ranges and phonic compass (e.g., the tenor pan's middle C and spanning over two octaves and the bass pan's low C and an octave and a half upward ranges) to some chosen motifs or components within a particular work—preferably from Trinidad and Tobago. But since the steel pan is now also a Caribbean music form, perhaps a work also from the region.[43] The effect of such an approach might foster a greater sense of inter-connectedness between the cultural forms within the region, varying disciplines, and scribal and oral texts. This dynamic way of perceiving the region's art would more truly represent the multifaceted, interdisciplinary and interwoven strands of the region's genres and traditions than the contemporary metropolitan-centered critical approaches which are often restricted in their outlook, confining the Caribbean crudely to general "ways of saying" that are fixed in other cultural paradigms.

By contrast, the approach which I postulate proposes an inward-looking orientation and procedure. The present preponderance of theory (usually the brainchild of the industrial centers and their universities) invariably has a way of fostering the types of criticism which are directly or indirectly metropolitan-looking. For example, in non-industrial but post-colonial worlds (like the Caribbean) theory and reading seem more concerned with metropoles than with inner worlds and inner cultures. The several brands of deconstruction, through their claims to subversion, necessarily imply and reinforce political and artistic inferiority—hence the need to focus on putting down, or deconstructing, some other. The reality of the inner worlds and inner cultures is that they possess their own particular potent cultural and artistic phenomena. Their potential need not be created by or for the succor of theory.

Within my approach, the act of exploration serves to bring clearer focus and form to these inner institutions. Explication and application solidify these inner institutions within the psyche, perception and consciousness of the uninitiated, in addition to legitimizing their cultural significance. As a Barbadian phenomenon, the tuk band and its music have been little researched. The ground work and exploration within the previous pages of this chapter attempt to bring the truth of its long and continued existence into sharper focus and to empower its cultural signification.

Within Brathwaite's concern with jazz, he stressed the realities of the actual Creole experience as evoking in representation "a form similar to that evolved by the American Negro in Jazz."[44] While one agrees with him that there is no West Indian jazz (in name), one might contest any suggestion that there is no Caribbean music of alienation and that ". . . the West Indian musical form, where it has any general area of application at all, is basically a music for dancing: a communal almost tribal form."[45]

In truth, Brathwaite refers mainly to the calypso as a point of contrast and reference (this perception is made prior to Brathwaite's own experiences in Jamaica in particular). But to generalize thus and otherwise about the Caribbean is to expose the frailty of such an approach. Furthermore, one does not wholly buy the idea that there is no suggestion of alienation or sense of chaos in calypso. For all of the psycho-social states of existence of the Caribbean person, there have been and continue to be concomitant musical structures and models of reflection and representation. I do not have to force the association between the tuk phenomenon and other facets of Barbadian cultural development and its present disposition—both band and nation are founded on West African orientations. Like the submerged, potent spirit of its native island, tuk has similarly served an underground, subversive existence. But both have thrived. Both have adapted. Both survive.

NOTES

1 Parry, Milman. "The Studies in the Epic Techniques of Oral Verse Making, I: Homer and Homeric Style." *Harvard Studies in Classical Philology.* (1930) 73-135.

2 Lord, Albert. *The Singer of Tales.* (Cambridge: Massiah, 1960).

3 See note 1 above.

4 Arant, Patricia. "Formulaic Studies and the Russian Bylina." *Indiana Slavic Studies.* (1967).

5 Benson, Larry. "The Literary Character of Anglo-Saxon Formulaic Theory." Publications of the Modern Language Association. (1966) 336.

6 Finnegan, Ruth. *Oral Literature in Africa*. (London: Oxford University Press, 1970) 518.

7 Anyidoho, Kofi, ed. *Cross Rhythms: Papers in African Folklore*. (Indiana: The Trickster Press, 1983) 25.

8 Ime Ikiddeh. "The Formulation of Critical Standards." *The Study of Oral Literature*.

9 Barber, Karin, ed. "Interpreting Oriki as History and as Literature," *Discourse and Disguises: The Interpretation of African Oral Texts*. (Edgbaston: Center of West African Studies, University of Birmingham, 1989) 13.

10 Finnegan, Ruth. *Oral Traditions and the Verbal Arts*. (London: Routledge, 1992) 29-32.

11 Ibid. 46.

12 Ibid. 46-47.

13 Kershaw, Baz. *The Politics of Performance*. (London: Routledge, 1992) 16-17.

14 See note 10 above. 44.

15 Ibid. 49.

16 Ibid. 50–52.

17 Ibid. 49.

18 Hall, Robert. *Acts Passed in the Island of Barbados 1643-1762*. (London, 1964) 113.

19 For example see *Parliamentary Papers*. Vol. 25 (London, 1826-7) 205-230.

20 Dickson, William. *Letters on Slavery*. (London: J. Phillips, 1789) 74-94.

21 Handler, Jerome and Charlotte Frisbie. "Aspects of Slave Life in Barbados: Music and its Cultural Context." *Caribbean Studies*. Vol. II (1972) 6-34.

22 Orderson, J.W. *Creoleana*. (London, 1842) 37-38.

23 Handler, J. and Frederick Lange. *Plantation Slavery in Barbados: An Archeological and Historical Investigation*. (Cambridge: Harvard University Press, 1978) 55-56.

24 See Dyott, W. *Dyott's Diary, 1781-1845: A Selection from the Journal of William Dyott*. (London: R. Jeffrey, 1907) 94-95; Alexander, J.E. *Transatlantic Sketches*. Vol. 1 (London, 1833) 158; Hughes, G. *The Natural History of Barbados*. (London, 1750)16-17; Oldmixon, J. *The British Empire in America*. Vol. 2 (London, 1741) 135.

25 Pinckard, George. *Notes on the West Indies*. Second Edition. (London: Baldwin, Cradock and Joy, 1806) 127.

26 Ibid. 264-265.

27 Collymore, Frank. *Notes for a Glossary of Words and Phrases of Barbadian Dialect*. (Bridgetown: Advocate Company, 1965).

28 The other indigenous Bajan rhythm is called *spouge*. It became recognized in the late 1960s as being associated with the Bajan Jackie Opel. This beat had a relatively short time of popularity in Barbados and throughout the Caribbean region. Throughout the 1970s it was a noted mainstay of the popular combos and brass bands of Barbados, and of the duo The Draytons Two. Nowadays it is a thing of curiosity and nostalgia in Barbados. It probably finds its most audible lifelines in gospel music, infecting the rhythmic and phrase stylings of some bands—paradoxically outside of Barbados. There is presently a concious drive by some Barbadian musicians to revive this music.

29 See note 2 above. 127.

30 John Oldmixon describes the playing of the Afro-Bajan's instruments as producing "a most terribly harmonious rhythm." See note 24 above. 134.

31 Roberts, Peter. "Interpretation in a West Indian Language Situation." *Carib No. 3 Perspectives in Language Aspects of Caribbean Creoles.* (1983) 92.

32 See note 21 above. 17.

33 Personal interview with Wayne "Poonka" Willock (June 1992). Poonka is a leading tuk band player in Barbados and an innovative composer at the forefront of incorporating indigenous rhythms into the calypso art form.

34 See note 33 above.

35 Hear the panoramic collection presented on the cassette *Indigenous Tuk Band Music* of Barbados by Ruk-A-Tuk International.

36 See the jacket cover of the audio cassette in note 35 above by Ruk-A-Tuk International.

37 See note 33 above.

38 "Foreday Morning," a term used to refer to early dawn, is a Bajan phrase not now in common or popular use, but which remains in the vocabulary of the elderly.

39 "Tuk Band Rhythm." A song performed in the early 1980s during the Crop Over Festival.

40 A true encounter, re-told by this writer's mother.

41 See note 33 above.

42 For example see Warner, Keith. "Calypso in Literature." *The Trinidad Calypso.* (London: Heinemann, 1982) 123-138.

43 See an enlightening introduction to this instrument, arguably the only significant twentieth century non-electronic musical creation. Noel, Terry and Jill Scargle. *Pan Play.* (Stoke-on-Trent: Trentham Books, 1988).

44 Brathwaite, Edward Kamau. "Jazz and the West Indian Novel II." *BIM.*(1967-68) 51.

45 Brathwaite, Edward Kamau. "Jazz and the West Indian Novel I." *BIM* (1967). 277.

2 CULTURAL INTERACTIVITY AND CARIBBEAN CRITICISM

LITERARY INTO CULTURAL STUDIES

In their theory-forming text, *The Empire Writes Back*, Ashcroft, Griffiths and Tiffin outline four models for reading what they call post-colonial texts. They refer to national, regional, race-based, comparative and syncretic-comparative models. Their book falls into the latter category, in which they offer a theory on all post-colonial texts based on the notions of language abrogation and appropriation. Much of their theorizing proceeds with the aid of linguistic phenomena towards highlighting the possibilities inherent in the "otherness" of post-colonial literature's linguistic "sign." To the European colonizer or "center," the colonial world is peripheral, relegated to the position of "other," or insignificant. Post-colonial theory which is a response (supposedly) to the center suggests that what the European ideology considers as insignificance is really difference. Therefore, Caribbean variations of a European standard language are not deficient but different. It is because of this particular difference that its words or "linguistic signs" hold the possibility for subverting the relationship between Europe and its insignificant "others."

Arguably, they owe more of their insight than has yet been acknowledged to the work of the linguists and others like Mervyn Alleyne,[1] Richard Allsopp[2] and Macpherson Nken Auike.[3] Their achievement, however, must be the attempt to forge a theoretical method of analyzing all post-colonial texts. Particularly in relation to the Caribbean context, theirs is really only a reworking of socio-linguistic theory, political history (much like the commonwealth literature movement) and post-Modernist rhetoric to add to an already existing body of literary, theoretical and critical materials. Lamming's counter-tradition (prospero/caliban) in Pleasures of Exile and Walcott's reworking of the Defoe myth/archetype have been offering similar theories of colonial counter-discourse for a long time. On this matter, Edward Baugh's conclusion to "Belittling the Grate Tradition in Good Humour," in which he cites such Caribbean examples as supporting the Empire, is much flawed and needs to be reversed to accord primacy to the Caribbean initiative.[4]

It was with the arrival of Edward Kamau Brathwaite's *Rights of Passage* (1967), *Masks* (1968) and *Islands* (1969) that a new perception was required within Caribbean verse. He would be the first Anglo-phone scribal-oriented poet to reflect a total confidence in and commitment to indigenous artistic resources. It is with Brathwaite first that there is a significant interplay in verse between the region's oral and scribal movements.

The movement of the oral-oriented tradition towards the scribal came most noticeably with Louise Bennett, who had been performing for some time before she came to prominence, surprisingly, in print. She is a forerunner in the scribal-oral interplay in Caribbean art. Others, such as Paul Keens-Douglas, would follow demonstrating greater flexibility between their oral and scribal texts, as Mervyn Morris contends of Keens-Douglas, ". . . in verbal detail, they [the scribal texts] are often quite different from the performances. They are not fixed to the degree of, say, a Louise Bennett poem."[5]

What Dalhatu Muhammed says of Hausa song is true of the poetry, song and related arts of the Caribbean as well. There are "more areas of oral influence on the scribal than vice-versa."[6] The extent to which the region's oral artists are influenced by the scribal tradition must be noted. There are the examples of Bennett and Keens-Douglas, who, although they are oral-centered performers, are to some degree committed to having their work appear in print. In addition, for dub-poets Michael Smith and Linton Kwesi Johnson, it is not uncommon to see their work in print. Adisa Andwele (who wrote and performed for some time as Mike Richards), the rhythm poet from Barbados, attempts to continue this trend of "total art." In the calypso world, the demands or vogue of the modern market now foster the printing of lyrics on the cover of record jackets and CD inserts. Jeanette Layne-Clark, the Bajan folk writer, is an interesting study in this regard. Though her creations are predominantly performance pieces, they were often featured in the national newspaper, *The Advocate*, at least once every week. I will make some other important comments in relation to this practice and its dynamics in the next section.

The oral and scribal movements in the contemporary Caribbean are more closely and intricately interrelated than the critical literature might suggest. This fact approximates the ends to which much of Gordon Rohlehr's criticism logically leads:

> The new wave of writers is not as easily divisible into distinct categories . . . . They have approached their heritage with a freedom rarely found in the pre-Independence era, seeking all available metaphors, sounds, rhythms and levels of sound and prosody. . . . as the situation demanded writers varied freely along the continua between folk and Modernist, creole and standard, oral and scribal . . .[7]

The development of the arts over the recent decades in the Caribbean attests to the level of this relationship. The wider recognition of interconnectedness points the way towards a more dynamic theory of orality in the Caribbean and offers new ways of conceiving and perceiving the region's art.

This meeting of traditions which Brathwaite's work embodied was a reflection of the times. His verse represents his diverse experiences. The effect which poets of the Modernist movement, like Ezra Pound and particularly Eliot, exerted on the region was quite significant. Both of these poets reacted to what they saw as society in stasis. Pound's "Cantos" and Eliot's "Wasteland" and "The Hollow Men" were direct responses to their particular situation and their treatments held even wider consequences and implications. Walter Sutton, on describing Pound's method as eclectic, goes on to add that he had drawn upon a "great variety of past cultures for spokesmen and examples of the values he wishes to promote."[8]

His method of cultural-historical hybridization was an interesting model, but it was Eliot's attitude towards his material and
his conversational tone (heard in broadcasts on the radio) that
effected the youthful Brathwaite.[9] Even so, the greater influences
on Brathwaite may be attributed to his experiences in Cambridge
and in Ghana—each an epitomizing symbol of two cultures and
modes of artistic expression, the former almost exclusively scribal
and the latter predominantly oral.

The Arrivants became Brathwaite's artistic embodiment of his
own historical and literary theories, as is revealed in such essays
and texts as "Sir Galahad and the Islands,"[10] "Jazz and the West
Indian Novel,"[11] and *The Development of Creole Society in Jamaica
1770-1820.*[12] *The Arrivants*' integrative treatment of history,
language and culture demanded a new critical method distinct
from the "New Criticism" which, according to Cliff Lashley, had
entrenched itself in West Indian literature. This transformed
criticism would have to be expanded and re-oriented to take
account of the oral elements which were vital to the region's
literature. From as early as 1967 Brathwaite attempted to
show an avenue of approach. In "Jazz and the West Indian
Novel" he attempted:

> . . . to show that a very necessary connection to the understanding of
> nation language is between native musical structures and the native
> language. That music is, in fact, the surest threshold to the language
> which comes out of it.[13]

Over a decade later, Brathwaite still bemoans the absence of
formal literary criticism on the oral movement in Caribbean
literature:

> In terms of more formal literary criticism the pioneers have been
> H.P. Jacobs (1949) on V.S. Reid, Mervyn Morris (1964) on Louise
> Bennett and most of Gordon Rohlehr's work, beginning with "Spar-
> row and the language of calypso" (1967). And that is all we have to
> offer as Authority, which isn't very much, really.[14]

There is more formal criticism going into the 1990s. Though
Brathwaite acknowledges the continuing scarcity of scholarship,
he cannot justify it.

> But, in fact, one characteristic of nation language is its orality. It is from "the oral tradition." And therefore you wouldn't really expect that large, encyclopedic body of learned comment on it that you would expect from a written language and literature.[15]

He does not specify why "you wouldn't really expect" this, but one can infer that he was making reference to the general situation of oral and scribal literature worldwide. Even so, this must not in any way continue to be the crutch which supports the absence of active, formal criticism on the region's oral traditions. If one should go further than Brathwaite has dared, the stark reality is that the greater body of critics of Caribbean arts have only recently come to respect and acknowledge its oral and music components as a true and deserving part of the tradition that in the universities is often called West Indian Literature. A popular mood in academia for a long time has been that orature and music are best left to the other disciplines of anthropology, ethnomusicology, folklore and cultural history. There continues to exist the uncertainty and ineptitude which surrounds the question of how to incorporate the oral and music components into the domains of the scribal canon.

I have made the point that the popular arts have been marginalized by the critical establishment for a long time in the Caribbean. Because there exists an uncertainty in possible methodology for the assessment and appraisal of Caribbean music and orature, I want to demonstrate one particular approach which represents a close reading of Gabby's "One Day Comin Soon."

It is surprising that such conscious compositions as Gabby's "One Day Comin Soon," with its message of redress and redemption, have not made their way into anthologies of Caribbean verse. When one weighs the power, popularity and sheer craft of such song-poems, there can be no logical, legitimate justification of other less deserving compositions being cited—other than some deficiency in criteria for selection or in the selectors themselves.

Although I have drawn particular attention to the song-poem "One Day Comin Soon," there are other equally deserving compositions by Gabby which come to mind (i.e., "Calypso," "Slavery Done," "Mulatto," "Culture" and "West Indian Politician"). There are numerous texts by other performers in the region which are equally deserving of mention and treatment by anthologists and critics. Red Plastic Bag's "We Must Rebuild," Pep's "Our Heroes," and Short Shirt's "The Fire Coming After" are but a few.

Apart from its strength as a musical and performance text, "One Day Comin Soon" can stand on its own as a scribal text. It stands up to close critical literary scrutiny and analysis.

Dey criticizing Nicaragua
Dey criticizing Ayatollah
Dey criticizing Cuba Angola and even Jamaica
Dey can't see de coal in dey own eye
Dey can't help but tell de people lie
Dem ain't know you shouldn't victimize
Dey so unwise ask Eric Fly (Dat's why I say)

(chorus)
One day comin soon de people will wake up
One day comin soon de people will shake up
And when they do, I'm tellin you
It will be heat on de tormentor's feet
(Jack) we got dem bawhling crawling
Sliding even hiding
Beggin we to ease de weight
But it will be too late

Dey workin hard against de people in dey political cathedral
Dey practicing destruction dishonesty is dey salvation
De people fed up wid they clap-trap de workers looking for a new gap
De youths searching now for another hat to put on dey head
Cause theirs feel like lead (that's why I said)

Tell dem I see a new Day dawning uh giving dem an early warning
'Cause in this final action de people voices will all rise up as one
And if they continue to malfunction I can see destruction on the horizon
An' it will not be de mass population who will feel de blast
It will be de ruling class (so fast)[16]

This song was composed and first performed in Barbados in 1984. Its theme of working class liberation and broad textual reference made it appropriate in other Caribbean and global contexts as well.

The song is logically presented. In the first stanza the poet introduces his argument. Succinctly put, his premise is that the political establishment in question is just as, if not more hypocritical and unjust, than certain other administrations in the world. The first stanza situates his discourse in a global geopolitical context. He refers to some of the then "trouble spots" in the world. He moves from the Middle East to Africa, then to the Caribbean, and finally to Barbados in the final line of the first stanza where the poet refers to the independent Bajan political activist Eric "Fly" Sealy.

The second stanza sets up the socio-political conflict as involving the political establishment versus "de workers," "de people" and "de youths." The third stanza presents a scenario of redress, with the pending uprising of "de mass population." The song is constructed so that it moves toward a climax, symbolized in the destruction of "de ruling class" in the final stanza.

The poem's chorus reinforces the threat of social upheaval. It portrays the imminent reordering of the society's present hierarchical class stratification. Throughout the chorus the poet juxtaposes two opposing movements. In contrast to the image of uprising associated with "de people" ("wake up" and "shake up"), the tormentors are presented as descending ("crawling," "sliding" and "hiding"). The poet then presents the final result of this social dynamic in the image of the masses on top asserting their rights and the ruling class shamefully "Beggin we [the masses] to ease de weight."

The poet's use of devices such as repetition and rhyme compliments the theme which he explores. The constant use of "dey" (they) places this poem in the rhetorical mode, characteristic of political speeches. This creates the tone and atmosphere which are essential to the success of this militant song-poem and enhances the effectiveness of his message. In a more practical sense, his use of the impersonal third person plural pronoun, "dey," to identify the oppressors is a device which serves to protect him from reprisals and his song from possible censorship. The most significant result of the poet's employment of enjambment is its effect on the poem's rhythm. The use of rhymes and half-rhymes has the effect of mirroring the sense of movement which is suggested by the song's theme. The poem's copious rhymes help to reinforce the sense of constant, rapid movement ("An' it will not be de mass population who will feel de blast/It will be de ruling class (so fast)." Note the following rhymes and half-rhymes: be and de, mass and blast, be and de, and class and fast).

The use of imagery is one of this song's most powerful technical components. In the second stanza religious imagery is used to explore the gravity of the society's present socio-political condition. The political establishment is presented as an entrenched, self-righteous band of miscreants in "dey political cathedral." This image of political sanctimony is continued in the following line, where the poet's choice of words is crucial and appropriate. Key words such as "practicing" and "salvation" take up the religious imagery and complete this stanza's symbolism ("Dey practicing destruction dishonesty is dey salvation.") The purpose and effect of this use of religious imagery is that it creates a more repulsive picture of the political leaders. They are presented as forming and fostering their own esoteric brotherhood—an order which is founded on the basic tenets of oppression and dishonesty.

The imagery employed in the final stanza is equally effective. The proximity of retribution is symbolized by the inevitability of the dawning of "a new Day." It is not the sun which appears in this "new Day;" it is "de people voices" which "all rise up as one." These voices loom "on the horizon" and in the "final action" affect a reaction of atomic proportions.

These are but some of the literary components which characterize many calypso compositions. Of course, the true reward of such compositions is in their performance with full musical accompaniment. But the calypsonian is very aware of the literary and technical aspects of his or her art form and, in more cases than we think, produces work which is valuable and satisfying in a number of varying forms, genres and media.

There remains a body of critics who are insensitive to the needs of the oral and musical movement. Where there might appear a fascination with orature, there is little active practice through in-depth study of the oral-musical component. A fuller appreciation of the region's potential in all spheres might come through a more balanced exploration of all its artistic resources.

Concomitant with Brathwaite's innovative first trilogy was a barrage of negative and even accusatory criticism. In hindsight this can be seen as attesting to the degree of disregard for Brathwaite's artistic fusion of the oral and the scribal traditions and his foregrounding of African-Caribbean culture. Richard Ho Lung pointed to Brathwaite's "exotic,"[17] fabricated world. Winnifred Risden pontificated that he "offers no message to the heart" because of its public rather than private nature.[18] And Derek Walcott got into the debate by inferring Brathwaite to be one of those "message-bearer[s] for the millennium" celebrating "the romantic darkness."[19] There was subsequently what has been termed the "Walcott versus Brathwaite" aesthetic debate.[20] While Walcott's poetry generally continued to reflect a propensity for the Euro-classical allusion, for Brathwaite there was a tradition no less classical which had existed in Africa for centuries but was largely unknown to critics.

For Brathwaite, the "great" English literary tradition had itself undergone many changes. He traces English develop-ment through Beowulf, Chaucer and the pentameter; the American movement with Whitman and others; and delves into the literary forms of the Caribbean where "the hurricane does not roar in pentameters."

> It is "nation language" in the Caribbean that, in fact, largely ignores the pentameter. Nation language is the language which is influenced very strongly by the African model, the African aspect of our New World/Caribbean heritage. English it may be in terms of its lexical features. But in its contours, its rhythm and timbre, its sound explosions, it is not English, even though the words, as you hear them, might be English to a greater or lesser degree.[21]

On the method, criticism and future of the Caribbean and its literature, Brathwaite writes:

I think, however that language does really have a role to play here, certainly in the Caribbean. But it is an English which is not the standard, imparted, educated English, but that of the submerged, surrealist experience and sensibility, which has always been there and which is now increasingly coming to the surface and influencing the perception of contemporary Caribbean people.[22]

Beyond Brathwaite and the critical stereotyping of the 1970s, the 1980s brought a number of positive responses to the need for new formal critical materials to include orature, music and performance. These can be found in the works of Gordon Rohlehr, Maureen Warner-Lewis, Carolyn Cooper, Michael Gilkes and Melvyn Morris. Glyne Griffith, an avid Caribbean academic in the sphere of literary theory, sums up the schools of contemporary West Indian literature as reflecting "two general approaches to the literary text" (I presume that his definition of literary text is all inclusive). He summarizes by stating, ". . . one approach tends toward the formalist school, and the other displays a socio-historical slant."[23] His corollary statement underscores the dangers of excitedly giving over to the present fad of imposing "theory" on all literature. He cautions, "Of course such generalizations run the risk of obscuring particular subtleties and nuances of critical emphasis . . ."[24]

It is exactly the existence of such particular subtleties in the region's national cultures which must raise suspicion of any all-embracing theory that effects a simplification of the region's arts—as such theories that underlie the construction of *The Empire Writes Back*. There is too much going on deep within the arts of the Caribbean and facile theorizing invariably submerges. So again, I contend that the procedure towards a fuller understanding of the Caribbean's culture and arts lies in the type of specialized works being undertaken within national contexts. These procedures are in need of expansion.

Calypso Judging Performance

Although a close reading of a calypso was performed in the previous section as a means of demonstrating possible ways of approaching such art forms within "formal" contexts, genres such as the calypso demand other criteria for total assessment. The practice of judging calypso at competitions reveals some of these other criteria. However, contemporary calypso judging is inadequate in a number of ways.

Throughout this century, the calypso art form has been offering methods for assessing the oral and music performance text. The art of judging calypso presents what must be the most rigorous, demanding and skillful of tasks. It is from here that any formal concept of Caribbean oral theory must turn for much of its substance. In his article on "Judging Calypso,"[25] Kendel Hippolyte explores the areas for assessing the calypso—its lyrics, presentation, melody, originality and arrangement. Such is the general guideline throughout the Caribbean, though the emphasis on the several categories is a source of much theoretical contention (as Hippolyte's article itself attests) and varies from country to country. In 1995 St. Lucia was experimenting with a system which gave greater weight to originality. In 1997 Barbados' calypso seemed to beg for the inclusion of this category. In the Calypso-related art forms lies a crucial, though neglected, aspect of the formal theoretical discourse on Caribbean oral art and performance.

In this section I want to take a brief look at the calypso art form, and more particularly, its form within the context of calypso competition. I will examine some of the practices of this particular performance event. I will raise a number of questions concerning the procedure, methodology and general signifying process which the present practices of kaiso competitions assume. I will briefly attempt to situate the discursive practices of competition in relation to certain theoretical perspectives which have to do with oration, discourse analysis, performance and ethnopoetics.

The phenomenon and practice of calypso competitions hold a number of implications for application of oral and performance theory in a broad sense. The "finals night" judging context is that occasion on which the merits or demerits of a particular composition and its performance are assessed. From what is frequently communicated about the process of judging, the act of judging is bracketed within the parameters of the performance night in question solely.

Like other commentators, I am inclined to suspect the claim to authority of this procedure, as I doubt that it affords the opportunity for the type of in-depth scrutiny, analysis and critique which audiences are asked to believe is endemic to the judging process. The legitimacy of this judging procedure derives its authority from traditional calypso practice.

At some "finals nights" of judging in contemporary situations, judges are known to sit between thirty to forty meters away from the stage and its performers. To my mind, this distance represents a vast space and suggests a break within the signifying process between performer and audience (judges). It is true that all performance events and contexts are constituted by space, but I contend that any attempts at appraising a performance, especially in depth, should be very concerned with mediating this space. Some of the interference which can accumulate over distance should be minimized by ensuring a more immediate discursive field between performers and judges.

In saying all this I am suggesting that in order to perform a complete appraisal of a performance like kaiso, the appraiser should be able to observe such signs as a performer's facial expression. These details are integral components of the signifying process. They should be considered simultaneously with other aspects of the performance. I question whether these intricate signs are indeed treated as important to the performance of kaiso. It is clear that a performance-centered reading of "finals night" competition is at odds with some contemporary judging practices.

The capacity of an individual to thoroughly analyze the lyrics, melody, rendition and other components of performance simultaneously within a five minute performance is a controversial issue in need of address. My immediate reaction is that it is surely possible to do a reasonable analysis of a song within this framed context. However, I question the impression of thoroughness which the art form, through its judges, claims for itself subsequent to some performance events. What I believe judges should seek to convey is the relative thoroughness of their own performance.

I am skeptical about the claimed thoroughness of calypso judging practice within its present format; I believe that judges are no more sure. In spite of an assertion that each performance event is bracketed by the entry and exit of the performer from stage, I am of the belief that this is not so in actual kaiso practice. Since judges are bound to hear recorded versions of song texts even before they actually judge them, they are also inclined to pre-analyze these songs. While some commentators might decry the bias which this process of prior analysis could create, I suggest that it can be viewed in another way.

A performance-centered view of the contemporary calypso judging format points to the limited and limiting contextual scope which the present process allows as constituting the performance in kaiso practice.

How can a song which has taken on significance within the public domain (outside of "finals night" context), somehow cease to "mean" and abandon its prior signification when transferred to "finals night" in a calypso competition? Why should one deny that he or she has heard and analyzed a text prior to the official judging? If there is an imperative to create a non-biased situation in terms of judging, then perhaps these competition events should ensure that the judging moment presents the first performance of all the songs which are to be judged (though even this method could create other problems).

Whereas Parry and Lord have stressed the importance of composition and performance, I have not given much attention to this consideration here since I think there has been much prior analysis of the relationship between the calypsonian and the calypso singer. I only want to link this discussion with the Parry-Lord oral theory by suggesting that their theory has greater application within traditional calypso practice. I am speaking of a tradition in which the composer is also the performer. I am also speaking of a particular type of performance—one in which the performer composes on the spot.

In contemporary practice the act of composing calypso is, for the most part, a self-conscious art. Although calypso is an oral performance art form, it becomes scribal at the point of composition when the composer commits it to the page. Therefore, I suggest that there is a need to re-examine the relationship between such oral forms and the scribal process. Given the fact that many composers are dependent on the written word when they compose (i.e., they sit with pen and paper), there is the sense in which they consciously negotiate the inter-textual space between thought and visible script. This draws further attention to the practice by such composers of approximating what are considered to be the oral formulaic components of calypso. By this I am referring to the tendency by such composers to internalize the formula of calypso and approximate them in the scribal form. Hence, many composers are cognizant to the utilization of repetative phrases, rhyme and national language which they know constitute the text of calypso. The point is that it is indeed easy to mimic the style of calypso's oral components. Contemporary calypso composition is primarily an ongoing process of this kind. A study of the art form's signifying process must take this fact into consideration.

Within the calypso art form the audience has always played a significant role. In contemporary practice, the audience's role during the performance continues to grow in terms of influence and importance. The measurement of their increasing influence, and specifically in relation to competition calypso, might be drawn from the influx of "party-type calypsos" within most performance events. In Barbados throughout the latter half of the 1980s, and now true in Trinidad and St. Lucia, audiences have insisted on having a show in addition to a competition They have simultaneously been insisting (though unknowingly) that the formula for judging the calypso text in total be revised and expanded to accommodate the more transgressive calypso performance. This is the type of calypso which challenges preconceived notions of a "real" calypso.

As the imperatives of market forces demand the transformation of the calypso, one is bound to witness a series of adjustments in terms of the criteria which are being used to judge the calypso. Presently, with the emphasis on rhythms in excess of 130 beats per minute, the art form has been re-negotiating its textual practice by laying lyrics of social commentary on top of these commercial-sounding tracks.

I think it is apparent that music genres in the Caribbean are susceptible to the dynamic shifts and imperatives of the international industry. Any analysis which seeks to engage the region's music forms at the level of theory must relate not only to national, social, cultural and aesthetic demands, but also to the impact of external and transnational forces within the music industry today.

NOTES

1 Allyene, Mervyn. "Acculturation and the Cultural Matrix." *Pidginization and the Creolization of Languages*. Edited by Dell Hymes. (Cambridge: Cambridge University Press, 1968) 169-186.

2 Allsopp, Richard. "How Does the Creole Lexicon Expand?" *Theoretical Orientations*. Edited by Valdman and Highfield. (New York: Academic Press, 1980) 89-107.

3 Auike, MacPherson Nken. "Code Switching as a Strategic Device." *Critical Theory and African Literature*. Edited by Ernest N. Emenyonu. (Ibadan: Heinemann Educational Books, 1987).

4 Baugh, Edward. "Belittling the Grate Tradition in Good Humor." Paper presented at the Ninth Annual Conference on West Indies Literature, 1990.

5 Morris, Mervyn. "Paul Keens-Douglas: It's Not Easy At All, At All, At All." Paper delivered at the Ninth Annual Conference on West Indies Literature, 1990.

6 Muhammed, Dalhatu. "Interaction Between the Oral and the Literate Traditions of Hausa Poetry." *Comparative Approaches to Modern African Literature*. Edited by S.O. Asein (Ibadan: Ibadan University Press, 1982) 41.

7 Rohlehr, Gordon. *Introduction to Voice Print*. (Essex: Heinemann, 1989) 11-12.

8 *Critical Essays on Ezra Pound*. Edited by Walter Sutton. (New Jersey: Prentice-Hall Inc., 1963) 3.

9 Brathwaite acknowledges Eliot's influence in *Contemporary Poets of the English Language*. Edited by Rosalie Murphy. (London: St. James Press, 1970) 129.

10 Brathwaite, Edward Kamau. "Sir Galahad and the Islands." *BIM* (1957) 25.

11 Brathwaite, E.K. "Jazz and the West Indian Novel." *BIM* (1967-68) 44-46.

12 Brathwaite, E.K. *Development of the Creole Society in Jamaica 1700-1820*. (Oxford: Clarendon Press, 1971).

13 Brathwaite, E.K. *History of the Voice*. (London: New Beacon, 1984) 16.

14 Ibid.16-17.

15 Ibid.

16 "One Day Comin Soon." First performed in 1984. Released on the album *One in De Eye*.

17 Ho Lung, Richard. "Sinner, Fame Priest Raps on God and Culture." *Caribbean Contact*. Vol. 2, No. 9 (December 1974) 19.

18 Risden, Winnifred. "Review of Masks." *Caribbean Quarterly*. Vol. 14, No. 1 and 2, (March-June 1968) 145.

19 Walcott, Derek. "What the Twilight Says: An Overture." *Dream on Monkey Mountain*. (New York: Farrar, Strauss and Giroux, 1970) 4-8.

20 See Ismond, Patricia. "Walcott Versus Brathwaite." *Caribbean Quarterly*. Vol. 17, No. 3 and 4 (September-December 1971) 69. See also Baugh, Edward. *Derek Walcott: Memory as Vision: Another Life*. (London: Longman, 1978) 39.

21 See note 13 above. 10. Also see his updating on this in "Caliban's Garden." *Wasafiri*. No. 16. (Autumn 1992) 2-6.

22 See note 13 above. 13.

23 Griffith, Glyne. "Veiled Politics in West Indian Criticism." Paper presented at the Tenth Annual Conference on West Indian Literature (St. Augustine: University of the West Indies, June 5-7,1991) 1.

24 Ibid.

25 Hippolyte, Kendel. "Judging Calypso." *Lucian Kaiso*. 28-29.

PART TWO

3 MUSIC AND CULTURE IN THE TWENTIETH CENTURY

A PRECURSOR: BEFORE 1960

Listening to the dust-covered 1965 recording of Shilling's "Independence Our Only Goal" brings the link between Africa and the Caribbean—and especially Barbados—into focus. The song is a tribute to the father of Barbadian independence, the late Errol Walton Barrow. It is similar to some West African songs of praise:

> *Errol Walton Barrow is de man*
> *To lead de Bajan Nation*
> *Other leaders did not see de light*
> *And they make themselves alright*
> *Since God gave Errol de vision*
> *He is backed by we Bajans*
>
> *(chorus)*
> *Independence is our only goal*
> *Independence have to save our soul*
> *And we want no other leader but*
> *Errol Walton Barrow*
> *And we want no other leader but*
> *Errol Walton Barrow.*[1]

Of course, there are Bajan folk songs which predate the twentieth century. Coming into the twentieth century there was a wealth of folk songs related to social practices and political events. There were those which spoke of female and male relationships, death and obeah. There was an array of children's songs which often accompanied the antics of game play.[2] Raymond Quevedo[3] records the increasing influence which folk songs and particularly their melodies had on the development of the calypso tradition in Trinidad at the turn of the twentieth century.[4] Such influences included songs from the islands of Martinique and Jamaica in the north, and St. Vincent and Barbados much nearer to its home. Even into the early 1920s the tune "Sly Mongoose," which was reportedly derived from Jamaica some twelve years earlier, was being again popularized and ruled the bands as one 1923 report in the Port of Spain Gazette reflects:

> The majority of the general bands were heard with the refrain of "Sly Mongoose" or "The Neighbor Next Door" and it was really disappointing to find that there was the monotonous similarity of sound especially when one is cognizant of the wealth of variations which [to] calypsos [are] available.[5]

Gordon Rohlehr considers its re-emergence to be due to the introduction of the concept of calypso-parody around the time.

The 1930s, whose socio-economic and political climate climaxed in the labor riots of 1937, was a period of renewed restriction and hardship for the oral practitioners. This period gave birth to such folk songs as the Bajan riot song "Today Is A Funny Night." It was also the era which saw experiments in the calypso duet between the then emerging Roaring Lion and Atilla The Hun in Trinidad.[6] Picong and the art of extempore were explored to their fullest. This was an era of change. These transformations were lamented by some artists. Lord Executor of Trinidad, who two decades earlier had astounded many with his innovative adaptation of the English language to this oral art, now decried the transformations which were being affected:

Foreigners and strangers who visit our shore
would like to know of something unknown before
To hear some strange and native melody
To see some sight of unusual revelry
But when you present them with what they have heard

or what they already know, that is absurd
you could never tickle their bone
When you give them the drum and saxophone.[7]

Spoiler and Kitchener, both emerging in the middle of the 1940s, moved away from the chronicle-type calypso which apportioned much emphasis on the war and depression. These calypsonians would dwell in the realm of calypso fantasy. In Kitchener's case, and especially upon his return from England, there would emerge what is perhaps the most successful collection of popular hits, also known as road marches, within the contemporary calypso era of the twentieth century. Most assessments of road march contributions begin with Kitch and Sparrow. There is a need to re-orient and rewrite much of this since the prior contributions of people like Roaring Lion should be highlighted more. This is a telling absence in the literature on calypso.

Around the islands, the prolific Mighty Terra was stamping his authority around St. Mary's College in St. Lucia, ruling as Calypso King from 1957-1967.[8] The Mighty Shilling and, later, Charmer were faced with much opposition in their ultra-conservative Barbadian society.

Throughout these other islands, as in Barbados, there was no umbrella organization for the popular oral and musical art forms. By 1956 St. Lucia would have their carnival committee and an attempt at organizing calypso competitions in Barbados would follow in about three years, but these would not achieve marked levels of national significance until the 1970s. Street corner performers such as the Vincentian Piti Quart had his Bajan equal in the Mighty Shilling. Roving cantors such as Shilling were, for the most part, freelance artists. With the guitar as the only accompaniment for his voice, Shilling was a regular welcomed and unwelcome performer at many an informal gathering—from the rum shop to evening sessions of dominoes at street corners "wid de boys." He and his craft were often ridiculed by the establishment and the socially cultured, though his skillful playing and his witty satirical, impromptu songs could evoke a spontaneous reaction from the most austere of onlookers or passers-by. Shilling's virtuosity on the guitar is a quality which has seen him labeled as one of the nation's best folk guitarists ever. His most popular performance is a legacy of these difficult years for the Afro-folk art tradition in Barbados—it is a playful and witty rendition:

> *My dog love your dog*
> *Your dog love my dog*
> *And if our doggies love each other*
> *Why can't we?*[9]

Censorship has remained a major concern for the folk artist. The Mighty Sparrow surfaced and practiced in an era in the 1950s when:

> Censorship continued, becoming embedded in the minds of those who took on themselves the burden of protecting public morality . . . there was also the question of whether calypsos should be played on the radio during Lent, which was not resolved until 1967.[10]

Sparrow won the 1956 Calypso Monarchy with the suggestive calypso "Jean and Dinah." This would signal a process of contention which would continue until and beyond the decade of the 1970s, when he formally withdrew from competition:

> *So when you bounce up Jean and Dinah Rosita and Clementina,*
> *round the corner posing*
> *Bet you life is something they selling*
> *And if you catch them broken*
> *you can get it all for nothing*
> *Don't make a row, yankees gone*
> *Sparrow take over now.*[11]

Barbados was deprived of artists of long-standing acclaim such as Sparrow because of the society's ultra-conservatism. Whereas Sparrow was just another artist in a growing organized tradition, the Bajan oral and music-centered artist had no such clear cut legacy. Barbados' twentieth century singers, like Mighty Charmer (an impromptu artist of immense skill), would have to measure up to the calypso from abroad. The Bajan critical establishment always demanded that their kaiso was sung with a non-Bajan cadence, style and flavor. These pressures surely retarded the pace of development of this genre and associated folk forms in the island. Mighty Charmer reveals that:

> I actually get my publicity from the man on the street. That's right. The people on the street from rum shop to rum shop. In those days I used to get a little penny here and a little four cents there and so on. And I kept it up. I used to sing from rum shop to rum shop when the Saturday nights come. And the people used to look for me. You see, it was the man on the street that kept me going where calypso is concerned.[12]

The dominance of Protestantism in Barbados also meant there was less tolerance of such manifestations of Afro-Caribbean indigenous expression. This was in contrast to what was obtained in Catholic-dominated territories such as Trinidad. Harry Hoetink makes the point that the Catholic church, because of its more universalistic tradition and its weaker organization at the lower strata level showed a greater tolerance towards "heathen forms." Conversely, in Protestant colonies the churches were generally stricter in their demands to abandon such practices which consequently had to go underground.[13]

Up to the late 1970s, Barbados' most popular and accepted singers of folk and calypso were the band of local White singers—the Merrymen. Their image as tourist ambassadors was, for some, one reason for accepting their use of indigenous rhythms. The conversion to the belief in the deeper cultural significance of indigenous cultural forms was a much later occurrence in Barbados' development.

Within the early period of the twentieth century the folk song, tuk band, service-o-songs, free-lance practitioners, and religious song and ritual were the institutions and media through which the Barbadian music and culturescape was being shaped. Future research will further document and explore the role of pre-1950s popular bands like the Percy Green orchestra. This orchestra was a leading dance band which played swing and jazz, mamba and samba, and Caribbean popular songs—what in Barbados was called *banja*. It comprised such musical instruments as saxes, stringed bass, guitars and steel drums. It was made up of over ten members who performed from music sheets. Such bands as the C.B. Brown Band were the practitioners who performed at regular dances. The role of these bands within the dance and party scene in Barbados is a phenomenon which deserves further analysis (this is an area on which I intend to expand in my next extended study of Barbadian music and culture).

WHY SPOUGE DIED

In the 1980s Barbados experienced a marked growth within its music entertainment scene. Through an increased level of participation by musicians and others working within the arts, many developments within the industry were realized. There was a marked interest in and emphasis on greater professionalism. Music increasingly became associated with business. Musicians were avidly preoccupied with keeping abreast of the latest technology in terms of musical equipment.

Arguably, all of these developments in the industry have sprung from other factors. For example, it could be argued that the kinds of advancements within the music scene were merely a reflection of changes which were impacting the body social and politic of Barbadian society. Commentators are bound to make reference to the strides which were being made in other areas of the arts, as proof of a national cultural revival.

By the latter half of the 1970s, spouge as a beat was waning in popularity. It had been a lively indigenous music. The Jackie Opel creation had given rise to a core of local combos and brass bands. Spouge had also brought about the formation of bands from many parts of Barbados—from the Vibrations in the north to other groups like Super 8, who were based in St. Philip. These were the first spouge bands to employ all local horn men within their performance sets.

When referring to the development of the music industry in Barbados in the 1980s and thereafter, I contend that one must refer to the 1970s and engage with spouge and with spouge texts. Furthermore, it is imperative to situate the post-1980s transformations in the music and culturescape of Barbados within a much wider period. Mass appeal and mass participation, which we associate with the period of Barbados' greatest resurgence of musical artistic production in the 1980s, were signs of development that were already evident in the spouge era. I think the contribution of spouge to the development of Barbados' music and culturescape has been understated in past and present discourse.

Through the impact of spouge, the music scene in Barbados throughout the 1970s was alive with activity. Spouge created an avenue of expression for musicians. It influenced technological developments within the music and related sectors of the island. For example, whereas bands like the Troubadours would have begun by amplifying their sound through a single speaker amplifier, by the latter half of the 1970s groups were in possession of a complete ensemble and a set of speakers for different instruments. By this time most bands were employing separate speakers for their bass and rhythm guitars. The organ or pre-synthesizer was also growing in popularity and as some recorded spouge texts would reveal, it was showing signs of replacing the guitar in certain functions. In songs like Wendy Alleyne's "I Have a Thing About You," guitar and organ are used with equal insistence and they complement each other within the recorded track. In Mickey D's "Bet Yuh Life I Do," however, the organ comes to the foreground in the mix.

It can therefore be claimed that this genre created the necessary musical infrastructure which would later serve as a support base for the rise of other popular bands in the 1980s and for the later developments within calypso in particular. In addition, the spouge era is responsible for the induction and maturation of a number of musicians who would go on in the 1980s to make other important contributions to the music industry in Barbados. Performers like Tony Grazette, who sang with the Blue Rhythm Combo, continued to perform well into the 1980s, becoming a singer of calypso and making an indelible imprint especially around the middle to latter half of the 1980s. He brought to calypso a keen understanding of interaction between singer and band. His polished renditions and an impeccable vocal diction are features of his style which he acquired during the spouge era. A similar case can be argued for other artists like David Hunte.

Other musicians and performers whose exploits can be attributed to the influence and impact of the spouge era of the 1970s include Lou "Jiggs" Kirton, Bert "Panta" Brown, Antonio "Boo" Rudder, Desmond "Calabash" Campbell, Joseph Niles, Shirley Stewart, Norman Barrow, Wendy Alleyne, Anthony "Black Pawn" Blenman, Kinky Star, Smokey Burke, Mike Grovesnor, Winston Blackett, Winston "Sox" Welch, Mike "Adisa Andwele" Richards and Charles D. Lewis.

Therefore, Barbados approached the decade of the 1980s with a plethora of competent musicians, aspiring sound engineers, and eager producers. It is from this platform that the developments in the 1980s and beyond were built. There is no subsequent musical form after spouge within the island of Barbados which can claim an independent development. I am not making a special case for spouge (since all musical forms are born out of prior musical forms), but the real point is that the 1970s are more important within Barbadian music history than present day discussions acknowledge. The present state of indecision, vacillation and timidity within the music industry in Barbados in 1997 stems largely from a non-understanding of the island's music culture. By this I am referring to an ignorance of the overall dynamics—inclusive of past developments—within the music and cultural spheres, and as touching their ideological contexts. Many of the present problems with which the music market of Barbados is faced have their source in the past, largely in the spouge era.

It is important to come to terms with the politics of the spouge era. Why was there a burst of excitement within spouge and a sizable output of recordings in the early 1970s? Why was this process followed by a subsequent decline of the music form by the late 1970s? What were the forces at work within and outside of the island which sought to deny this musical innovation the status which it was quickly acquiring in the region? My final point in this regard is that presently the industry in Barbados has not learned from the spouge era. The haunting reality of this disclosure is that the industry is approaching that stage which the spouge era had found itself just before it contracted. Having stimulated an active interest at home and in the region, the nation and its entertainment industry appear very unsure about the next stage of progression into the international domain. I say "nation" because I am of the belief that in order to project a cultural item into the international sphere there is the need for a total national consciousness and effort. One wonders to what extent the demobilization of this national drive sounded the demise of spouge.

I support the view that the waning of spouge in the late 1970s can be more directly attributed to forces extrinsic to the music (i.e., socio-political, ideological and cultural factors) than to the music itself as a beat. There is a body of contention that says spouge as a beat lacked variety. Proponents of this viewpoint go on to suggest that the decline of spouge can be directly attributed to this fact. In an attempt to legitimize the claim that spouge was monotonous and suffered for want of innovation, advocates of this view refer to a number of motifs which characterized spouge. They refer to its syncopating drum pattern, its consistent strumming on the guitar, its ever audible cow bell (spouge tot), and a "lazy" disengaged bass. Although I agree that these motifs are characteristic of some spouge texts, I take issue with the suggestion that their presence in the music constitutes "monotony." Furthermore, I suggest that given the example of dancehall, there can be no direct correlation between recurring musical motifs and a claim of monotony (and by inference non-interest).

However, I do not want to engage the debate at that level. I do not intend to make a case for spouge by enlisting the dancehall idiom as a comparative referent. Rather, I contend that as lyrical, musical and performance text, spouge has been mis-critiqued in the popular discursive domain. I know of no previous extended academic critique of spouge in which there is any attempt to engage with the text in total as a way of situating this music art form within the Caribbean culturescape. I am, therefore, attempting to redress a number of critiques, as well as create a major discourse on the spouge text.

My contention is that whereas spouge music has been lumped together as being of one style and a certain treatment and purpose, the reality is that as a music in popular live and recorded practice, spouge has exhibited a number of varying sub-textual traits and developments. I want to demonstrate a number of ways in which spouge is diverse in musical practice, as there were a number of applications and interpretations of spouge during the 1970s.

In the public forum it was recognized that Cassius Clay attempted to popularize his style of spouge called "Dragon Spouge." Some reference has been made to the raw spouge of the Draytons Two. I want to take this process of sub-textualizing spouge much further by pinpointing other sub-textual trends in the music. References to the works I cite are based on these works as recorded texts. On very few occasions subsequent to this point do I refer to live performance.

I concede that the Draytons Two's style of spouge can be largely categorized as raw spouge, however, their recorded texts are not all to be lumped together as constituting a single style. For example, their "Blueberry Hill" and "G.O. Go" are markedly different from their "Play that Spouge Music" and "Written Down" in treatment and application. The former two songs are more labored in terms of tempo. As recordings they make use of heavy strumming, and the cow bell is in the foreground in both mixes. There is a detectable harshness to these mixes which gives them a forthrightness, indicating that these are spouge tracks in their more natural treatment. This is the way audiences at live events in the 1970s would most likely have experienced the sound of spouge.

"Play That Spouge Music" and "Written Down" represent a number of innovative applications of spouge. The single most noticeable difference about these two songs is that they represent what amounts to a transgressive performance, if only on account of their non-employment of the cow bell as an integral component of their text. In fact, it is bass and drum which play the leading part in the groove of both rhythms. The drum applications in these songs do not conform to the pattern which characterizes traditional spouge. Within "Written Down" are two snare shots just before the second beat of the bar, and a third snare falls in its usual place just before the fourth beat. There is a redefining of the relationship between the snare and foot drums. In "Play That Spouge Music" this pattern is reversed where one snare shot precedes the second beat in each bar and two shots precede the fourth beat. These represent transgressive applications of the drum in spouge. Furthermore, these two songs make use of the bass style of "popping" or "plucking." At the time of this application by Ricky Aimey, these performances did not constitute spouge to some individuals. This is an indication of some of the innovations which were being fed into spouge music by its practitioners and musicians. It is fallacious to talk of the Draytons Two's music as representing one type of spouge.

My analysis of a large number of recorded spouge texts from the 1970s shows a number of other diverse musical treatments within the art form. It is inaccurate to speak of 1970s spouge as defined by a particular guitar strum, the presence of the cow bell, and a "lazy" bass, when a survey of numerous spouge songs reveals a range of varying applications of these instruments. To be more specific, not all spouge songs have made use of these recurring motifs. The BRC's "Lonesome Me" does not employ a cow bell, but it is replaced by the rim shot. This same composition is exciting in its phrasing and employment of staccato inflections, accented effectively on the drums and punctuated by ambient horn riffs. In "Do You Like Sweet Music" the emphasis here is, again, squarely on musicianship and forcefully polished vocals. The musical text is not self-consciously reliant on the features outlined above as constituting spouge.

Other groups also were asserting spouge's performative difference. In "Let That Someone Be Me" the Hilltones strip spouge of a number of its percussive instruments and create a rhythm and blues inflection in the absence of those percussive components. In the Troubadours' "Are you Sure," they faded out the drums during verses to create tonal contrasts in the song. A group like the Sandpebbles were on the verge of pop-spouge in their composition "Some Day My Love." This recording makes overt use of voice effects. It is a well-tailored recording which takes on a commercial edge.

Horns added a textural richness to some spouge compositions. These horns were being used differently in a number of recordings. The Bimshire Boys' "Dance with Me" makes use of fat sounding horn riffs which are most effective for creating musical tension at the end of verses, in addition to stating the band chorus segment within the composition. Groups like The Organization and Super 8 featured trumpet solos and employed horns in call and response phrases. The BRC's application of horns on recorded texts draws attention to their centrality in the construction of BRC spouge—horns do not merely embellish but are dominant within many BRC mixes. It makes an even more interesting comparison to listen to the Organization's "Bye Bye Love," BRC's "Knock on Wood," the Escorts' "Talking 'Bout Music," Bimshire Boys' "Simple Song," and Super 8's "Come Back Girl" to compare the various treatments of horns in spouge.

Within the corpus of songs which were being performed in the 1970s there are a number of diverse stylistic and musical applications of spouge. Closer scrutiny reveals other distinctions and experiments in terms of tempo, instruments used, subject matter, vocal character, tonal and intonational registers, harmony, effects processing, fusion, crossover, over-dub track mixing, and improvisation.

In a previous paragraph, I made reference to the Sandpebbles' "Some Day My Love." Its voice effects enhance the overall presence of the musical production. But I want to call attention to other songs and their singers who made an impact on audiences. I am referring to recordings which make use of less effects than in the Sandpebbles' track. I am of the opinion that one of the single most distinctive and addictive features of 1970s spouge music has been the virtuosity of many spouge vocal performances. Whereas many commentators have pointed to the "spouge tot" and other distinct musical motifs as situating spouge within the music and soundscape of Barbadian and Caribbean music, I suggest that spouge's staying power and popularity rested heavily on the strength of its vocal performances. Among the many songs that illustrate the type of performance I am speaking of are:

"Always Thinking of You" by Checkmates
"Here I am Baby" by Lunar 7
"Bet Yuh Life I Do" by Mickey D
"Simple Song" by Midge Springer
"So Nice To Be With You" by Solid Senders

To this list can be added many of the song texts cited in previous paragraphs, as well as most of the spouge songs performed by the likes of the Draytons Two and Wendy Alleyne. Developments in the Barbadian entertainment industry during the 1980s must be seen as coming out of this background of the 1970s. A substantial understanding and awareness of the musical and performance practices of the 1970s should predate any appraisal of what transpires later on in the 1980s and beyond. During the 1970s there was much interest in local bands. Clashes were a main drawing card at dances. The 1980s and calypso culture mobilization is often referred to as the period of the nation's greatest manifestation of an interest in its own culture within contemporary times. But, had conditions been similar in the early days of spouge, especially in terms of travel, transport and communication networks, then we might have seen a similarly large mobilization of the masses into certain performance spaces. It is fallacious, I know, to attempt to detect the level of public interest and support simply by gauging numbers and at one given venue. Anyone who attempts to gauge the level of national support and fervor for spouge during the 1970s must pay attention to other indicators such as the attitudes of audiences to the music, the response based on attendance and participation at performance events, the degree and level of artistic creations which were being produced and performed and the volume of recorded texts.

The point to re-emphasize is that the spouge era was a forerunner to the more contemporary period of calypso, soca and ringbang in Barbados. Spouge music demonstrated that Barbados and Barbadians were capable of creating and sustaining a musical art form. Spouge created a national identity. Young primary school children of the mid-1970s practice approximating the syncopated phrasing of the spouge drums. This captured their imagination. BRC, the Opels, Vibrations, and the Check-mates were drawing crowds at fairs and other events. The teen idols were people like Mickey D. Bajans were singing spouge songs in everyday life. Spouge, the beat, was exported outside of the nation and throughout the Caribbean. As a marketable product, spouge in the 1970s reached the standard to which the Bajan kaiso would later climb within the early 1990s.

The demise of spouge must be explored in light of the indifference of the media towards the phenomenon, the disdain which the establishment demonstrated towards the Jackie Opel creation, and the absence of a consolidated approach to the development of the rhythm by those in the industry. These reasons, combined with a national ignorance in relation to the sociopolitical, ideological and economic value of cultural innovation, resulted in the disintegration of spouge culture.

What marks the 1980s as an important decade within Barbadian music and culture is the central role which the institutionalization of crop over and kaiso played. The post-1980s period was one of numerous technological advances and musical experimentation at the national level. This was the era of synthesizers, sequencers, drum machines, multi-track home studios, and the synthesizing of musicians to the workings of the industry at home and, to a lesser extent, the international level.

Unfortunately, this study is not directly concerned with all the finer workings within the music industry in Barbados over the period which it treats. It focuses more on the calypso and centers the work of the artist Anthony "Gabby" Carter in the following chapter. This focus is rewarding in many regards. By bracketing its scope to a particular genre, this book is able to treat a single artist and his works in greater detail— something that more general studies would not be able to accomplish. It asks the reader to see the artist treated as being representative of a larger body of performers.

The advantages of doing a case study on Gabby are many. His involvement in folk as well as calypso means that this study engages in debate on the genres of folk, calypso, soca and other post-1990s hybrid forms. The association which he forms with Eddy Grant also means that the study must deal with the interactive tensions which are played out within his works. On the one hand, he is in tune with the calypso tradition; on the other hand, he has been working closely with Ice label's crossover machinery.

This study has not set out to be in-depth in terms of its approach to music in Barbados. It might be considered a first step in outlining some links between earlier practice and more contemporary developments within the musicscape of the island. Hopefully, future studies will look at the pre-1950 and pre-1980 eras in greater detail. Within the kaiso genre specifically, there is much scope for future studies on the great number of contemporary artists—Red Plastic Bag, Bumba, Grynner, Black Pawn and Observer—who make up the island's core of performers.

NOTES

1 Agard, Shillingford "Shilling." From a 1965 archival recording of his performance of the Panegyric "Independence."

2 *Traditional Folksongs of Barbados.* Edited by Trevor Marshall. (Bridgetown: MacMarson Associates, 1981). Also, listen to the Barbados Folk Singers' 1964 audio recording (Wirl 1006) of twelve traditional folk songs including the 1870s "Murder in De Market," "King Ja Ja" and "Pack She Back." Or listen to DaCosta Allamby's compositions of the 1940s and 1950s such as "Steel Donkey" and "Conrad," or to all the Bajan folksongs recorded by The Merrymen, especially throughout the 1960s.

3 Quevedo, Raymond. *Atilla's Kaiso.* (Port of Spain: University of the West Indies, 1983) 14–19.

4 Also see Hill, Errol. "The Trinidad Carnival: Cultural Change and Synthesis." *Cultures.* Vol. 3, No. 11 (France, 1976) 54–85

5 *Port of Spain Gazette.* (January 25, 1934) 7.

6 de Leon, Rafael. *Calypso from France to Trinidad: 800 Years of History.* (Port of Spain, 1988) 79-112.

7 Pitts, Harry. "Calypso from Patois to its Present Form." *Guardian Independence Supplement.* (August 26, 1962) 41–43.

8 See Ellis, Guy. "Remembering the Terra." *Lucian Kaiso.* No.1 (February 1990) 4.

9 "My Dog" was not composed by Shilling but he certainly stamped his own style on its text. The song "Too Late Corkie," which talks of crime and punishment, is also remotely familiar.

10 Rohlehr, Gordon. *Calypso and Society.* (Tunapuna: H.E.M. Printers, 1990) 315.

11 See *Sparrow the Legend.* (Inprint, 1968).

12 "Mighty Shilling." Replayed on CBC (November 1994).

13 See Hoetink, Harry. "The Cultural Link." *Africa and the Caribbean.* Edited by Graham and Knight. (Baltimore: John Hopkins Press, 1979) 29.

4   CENTERING AN ARTIST

GABBY AND THE ENTERTAINMENT INDUSTRY: 1950-1970

> I always used to tell my mother I am going to be a singer and she used
> to laugh and she used to say: "Why you don't learn ah trade? . . . show
> [me] one single successful calypsonian!" I couldn't![1]
>
> Anthony "Gabby" Carter

Anthony "Gabby" Carter was born in the environs surrounding
the city of Bridgetown, Barbados. He was born around 1950, an
era, as the above quotation reveals, when there was much hostility
towards and mistrust of the calypso singer, performer and the
local artist as a whole. An understanding of the contemporary
development of calypso and related musical forms within Barbados reflects an accompanying concern with the nation's cultural
and social renaissance.

The Barbadian calypsonians of the 1930s, 1940s and 1950s
were The Mighty Charmer, Shilling, Jerry and Lord Sivers.
There was a thin line of contact between these calypsonians and
what was then a more vibrant tradition in Trinidad and Tobago.
Charmer did performances with the likes of Kitchener. These
practitioners were inextricably bound to Barbados because, in
spite of the ridicule and rejection of their craft by a native
audience, there was also a more unfriendly and condescending
attitude toward their art by those who were the true exponents

from elsewhere in the region. There is much scope for an in-depth exploration of the life and times of such early and mid-twentieth century Barbadian artists. Resource persons and material on calypso are presently limited.

Even in early childhood, people would give the young Gabby "two or three cents to sing over calypsos by Lion and Kitch and so on."[2] His earliest encounter and fascination with calypso was acquired through listening to the gramophone. Owning a gramophone was a luxury at the time, as well as the only real way of claiming access to the latest music from the Caribbean (or from anywhere else in the world for that matter).

> There was a lady called Ms. Walcott who used to live next door to me who had a, a gramophone, which was the only gramophone we had in the whole village, and I used to get the chance to hear her play some of the old calypsos, people like Lion and Atilla, Tiger and Destroyer, people like that.[3]

Closer to home, the accessibility of other performers such as Charmer, Sugar, Lord Sivers, Mighty Romeo, Producer and Sir Don served to stimulate an innate fascination, love and admiration for the art form. When a young boy in Sunday School, Gabby was affiliated with the Chapman Lane Choir, a religious Christian singing group under the directorship of Mr. Seymore Blackman. He later sang under Mr. Dottin in the St. Mary's Choir. He mixed this formal practice with the more spontaneous evening public bath singing sessions with the boys who would subsequently form The Opels, a popular group of the 1970s. Gabby grew up listening to some of these performers and seeing Bajan Jackie Opel. Jackie was the consummate artist-as-singer and composer of many styles. Accomplished musicians, performers and dancers like Jackie Opel appeared at dances and other organized shows. Places such as the Drill Hall were regular venues for these shows and also featured a number of local combos that played rock steady, soul and calypso. But Gabby also saw Jackie Opel on less formal occasions. Gabby recalls a specific occasion when "the late great" came into Chapman's Lane to sing for a woman called Monica, a street performance that Jackie Opel accompanied with dance, which on this occasion became a kind of theater spectacle.

In spite of the financially and socially unkind ambiance associated with the sphere of the arts, Gabby's enthusiasm for singing, composing and performing grew. As those of the performing generation of the 1960s and earlier frequently attest, there was no such thing in those days as the rights of the artist. An artist was contracted and obliged to satisfy his or her audiences. Although the musical profession was undergoing transformations and modernization on the international scene, there was little advancement in Barbados. Washrooms served as dressing rooms. A complimentary drink and the generous tips of tourists and visitors were common incentives for the performer. According to artists of that period, many of those who stuck with the arts by singing, dancing or playing in a band did so because of a love, commitment and dedication for their craft. Mark Williams, a promoter from this era, cites the sense of accomplishment from having satisfied an audience as being an important incentive for many artists.[4] These were the conditions for some of the performers of Gabby's age and aspiration. Such an era is often looked back on nostalgically as the times of the artists' genuine concern for their craft and their development. The sheer devotion of those days is often compared and contrasted with the more contemporary preoccupation with commercial imperatives. A composer and performer like Gabby straddles this divide by being, on the one hand, considered a folk artist par excellence and, on the other, labeled a commercial affiliate of the internationally successful "superstar" Eddy Grant.

In reflecting on the connection which is often made between West and Central African singing poets, performers and their Afro-Caribbean descendants, the role and practice of Gabby presents an interesting study and critique of the tenets of such a legacy. Perhaps the last remaining identifiable vestiges of a link with some distant past and the tenets which that tradition holds most dear lie within such a performer.

As is expected, some introductions to the evolution of kaiso begin with a discussion of the origin of the terms *kaiso* and *calypso*. Keith Warner's summary of the several theories on the origin of the words is useful for further reading.[5] Most commentators favor the theory stating that the term which describes this art form is derived from the Hausa word *kaito*, a cry of approval. For Raymond Quevedo (Atilla the Hun) the term *kaiso* evolved until it became *calypso*.[6] Errol Hill supports this view in *The Trinidad Carnival*.[7] Roaring Lion's *Calypso From France To Trinidad* proposes that the origins of calypso are found in the ballade, a verse form popular in northern France around the thirteenth century. Most academic critics ignore Lion's findings, but it is imperative that serious and honest consideration be given to his hypothesis.

This book tends to privilege the view that rhythmic forms such as kaiso have their origins in African songs of ridicule, praise and blame. Such African songs feature call and response structures, and are improvised. The numerous historiographic descriptions of similar types of songs in the New World can support the theory of the kaiso as having some roots in Africa. Texts such as Dina Epstein's *Sinful Tunes and Spirituals*[8] and Roger Abrahams et al's *After Africa*[9] provide the most comprehensive and copious collection of New World examples which lend support to this concept of musical continuities.

It is on the island of Trinidad where the practices now associated with the kaiso art form were most notably formulated and organized at a national or quasi-national level. Gordon Rohlehr traces the nineteenth and twentieth century development of kaiso through songs associated with dances such as Jhouba, Bel Air and Bamboula.[10]

This book cannot do justice to the evolution of kaiso in Trinidad. Kaiso's development is not a primary concern of this book. Rohlehr's *Calypso and Society in Pre-Independence Trinidad* provides a comprehensive outline of that aspect of kaiso's development. John Cowley's 1992 Ph.D. dissertation, "Music and Migration,"[11] is also a valuable document in this regard. The development of the kaiso and the other song forms of Barbados is less well documented. Apart from the Marshall folk song collection and other journalistic articles, there are no other major scribal documents devoted specifically to Barbadian music in the twentieth century. There have been seventeenth, eighteenth and nineteenth century European visitors to Barbados who have recorded descriptions of music and related practices; these are arguably the earliest accounts of Barbadian music. I have referred to some of these works in Chapter One.

The Barbadian dance and music called the "Joe and Johnny" is a parallel form to some of the dances which Rohlehr associates the early practice of kaiso.[12] What other information there is on kaiso in Barbados in the first half of the twentieth century is sketchy, and based largely on undocumented oral sources.

Shilling and Charmer are perhaps the two most notable Barbadian oral performers in the kaiso tradition in the pre-1950 period. As noted above, they and other performers like themselves had occasional interactions with the more organized and vibrant tradition in Trinidad. For example, a 1908 *Trinidad Mirror* article refers to "a native of Little England" who was part of the Trinidad Golden Star band which eventually won the singing competition that year. The report observed that "this son of Bimshire had more adjectives and adverbs at his disposal . . . no matter whether they were misused or not."[13] Some Barbadian songs were popular in Trinidad and were renamed and performed by well-known Trinidad kaisonians. For example, the Belasco band's 1914 "Buddy Abraham" and "Little Brown Boy" are songs which emanate from Barbados. The latter song had been popular in Trinidad in 1910.[14] The Bajan song "Murder in de Market" was performed in 1939 by kaisonian Houdini and renamed "He Had it Coming." Bajan-born Lionel Licorice released a number of songs in the islands from abroad. "Baijian Girl" and "I Has The Blues For Thee Barbados" were two of his 1912 compositions. The releasing of songs on record by a Bajan at that time was not a common practice by any means.[15]

There also seemed to be an influence on the Trinidad kaiso by what one 1923 *Weekly Guardian* report refers to as "the familiar music of the reed and steel of the adjacent colony of Barbados."[16] This is clearly a reference to the Bajan tuk band. It is an indication that the rhythms of tuk were being felt beyond the boundaries of its practice in Barbados.

In the same way that Lord Melody of Trinidad was a regular singer in rum shops,[17] the majority of Barbadian singers of kaiso performed at these venues. Unlike his Trinidad counterpart who was spotted by another established talent (Lord Invader) and contracted to sing in a more professional context, the aspiring Bajan artist did not have these avenues for advancement. There was no established network of performers. So the Bajan kaisonians continued to sing at street corners, parties or dances of friends. Their performances were largely informal and their practice was viewed as a pastime activity rather than a serious profession. As happened with the tuk band, kaiso singers performed on holidays and other related occasions. They sang popular songs from other islands as well as their own compositions. For example, Shilling places his song "Too Late Corkie" as a 1924 composition:

One night I was a sleeping and uh heard yuh lamp
Corkie call Ambrazine
she say wha happen wid you come wid me
de white man got de money
Ambrazine turn and she went right down
down by Kensington ground
before she could wink or even think
duh had her floor to de ground

(chorus)
Too late oh Corkie too late
too late oh Corkie too late
too late to contemplate
five years isn't fourteen days.
Too late oh Corkie too late
too late oh Corkie too late
too late to contemplate
five years isn't fourteen days

Lorise get up and he beg fuh dem
he say ma lord they are mortal men
he say I know dat is dat
and dat is why I ain't give dem de cat
they only can serve de time[18]

Bajan kaisonians of the early and middle twentieth century are remembered for their impromptu performances. In this regard,

Gabby cites Charmer and Lord Radio as "impromptu artists of great skill."[19] In the same way that tuk band players were categorized as drunkards and lighthearted performers, these Bajan kaisonians and their songs were deemed to be immoral, common and sinful by the establishment and upper classes.

An important outlet for performers such as Lord Radio was the hotel industry. Tourism provided an avenue for singers to perform Caribbean songs and their own compositions to visitors of the island. Dances on weekends at popular venues, especially around the city of Bridgetown, provided the opportunity for performers to entertain others and make money. However, few of these artists could depend only on singing and performing for their livelihood, for there was not much money to be had from these performances. When Gabby made his entrance into the practice of singing kaiso in the early 1960s, this was the type of fragmentation which characterized the singing art and profession in Barbados.

Gabby's formal induction into the art of calypso (if there is any specific occasion) was signaled when he competed in the then privately sponsored 1965 calypso competition. It is important to understand that within the tradition of the calypso, and as it evolved and developed throughout the Caribbean, formal competition has been an important component. I referred to this earlier in Chapter Two. In these competitions, each artist's skill, craft and performing abilities are matched against the other's. Within the modern structure of calypso competitions throughout the region, there is an elimination process which reduces a field of scores of singers to a mere eight or so performers. These finalists then engage in an "all-out battle" before some eight judges and thousands of others (the audience), who themselves are no less qualified to judge, and who do in fact individually and collectively sound their pronouncements during and after a performance event.

In 1965 when Gabby, then sixteen years old, entered his first competition, he would sing one composition as was then customary, as opposed to the more contemporary practice of rendering two pieces. Within the calypso tradition each calypso singer usually chooses a sobriquet. The sobriquet is important since it is supposed to epitomize some attribute of the calypsonian, for example, his boldness or forthrightness. Therefore, the names or titles of great, well-known or infamous personages, figures or animals are desirable (i.e., Atilla the Hun and Roaring Lion). There had never been any doubt in Gabby's mind about what would be his sobriquet. Coincidence brought the name "Gabby" to Anthony Carter in his youth and affixed a sobriquet to him. It came about during a give-and-take episode in his colonial classroom between giver-schoolmaster and the boy:

> I was in de class one day . . . I wrote something about him . . . I started singing, the man said . . . "why don't you learn the gift of gab . . . become an eloquent speaker" . . . I went and I checked out the word gabby and it meant a talkative or an eloquent speaker.[20]

When Gabby next entered the then intermittent calypso competition at the age of nineteen, he emerged as the winner over a number of singers—some of whom had been his mentors. One of his early compositions treated the topical phenomenon of the heart transplant. This song's persona, impersonating a surgeon, is certainly up to performing more than are the duties of this profession:

> *So he decided to take a chance with this operation*
> *Work it out on me girlfriend aunt (Lord)*
> *Carry she down by de cemetery*
> *Wid this long white knife in he hand*
> *Turn she 'round lays he down start de operation.*[21]

Gabby then embarked on an artistic and commercial odyssey abroad, performed on a series of cruise-tourist liners, and settled in the United States in 1971. It was undoubtedly through these experiences of contact with the larger world and its peoples and cultures that he would become more than a folk artist. Performing for tourists outside the confines of the local setting would prove to be a challenge when selecting material and to the performance skills of the songster. While in New York, he embarked on a career in theater with the Barbados Theater Workshop, for whom he not only acted but composed and performed the greater part of their musical scores. This professional experience in theater and stage has left a definite imprint on many of his performances. Apart from the charismatic-cum-spiritual aura which can loom over a one-on-one rap session with Gabby—an aura which is also present when he performs—there is always the sense that he is a shrewd master of theater. Gabby's ability to alter his material going into a series of improvised lines, enact the meanings of his lyrics, or alter the tone and contours of his voice for some desired effect successfully entrances his listener.

FOLK MUSIC AND CONTEMPORARY SOCIETY

Gabby's returned to Barbados in 1976 began a new era in his development as an artist. It marked the period of his steady involvement in the arts in Barbados as a composer, songwriter, performer and recording artist. To date he is without a doubt the most versatile and complete composing and performing talent on the island. (Although this section continues to focus on Gabby, there are other individual performing artists who have significantly contributed to folk music, i.e., Vernon Cadogan, Richard Layne and Johnny Koieman.)

To categorize and segment Gabby's works as this book does is not an indication that there is any strict austere distinction by the artist himself between what are effectively co-related and continuous genres. In his text *Negro Folk Music U.S.A.*, Harold Courlander recognizes the difficulty of conclusively defining folk music, "It is not likely that any over-all definition of the nature of Negro folk music could be stated . . . ."[22] This is a view which is echoed in the English context by Maud Karpeles.[23] In theorizing on the nature and the origins of folk songs, she divides the main schools of thought into two groups: the production and the reception theorists.

> Those of the production school of thought maintain that only those songs that have originated with the folk are folk songs. Those of the reception school hold that the origin is unimportant and that all songs that have achieved a wide currency among the people can be termed folk songs.[24]

But Karpeles goes on to propose that oral transmission is "the one overriding factor on which the making, and the nature of folk music depends."[25] Her analysis of the three processes which underlie the folk song—continuity, variation and selections by the community—is useful for creating a general idea of what characterizes the folk song tradition. However, I cannot totally endorse her ideas on the present day folk song. She holds the view that "to attach the term 'folk song' to a newly composed song, besides being erroneous, is injurious to the concept of folk song."[26] She believes that because of technology (e.g., the record) present day compositions are stereotyped, and, despite their popularity, can always be referred back to as the original. According to Karpeles, they then become "stultified."[27]

This is not always the case, as will become more evident throughout this book. The recording or printing of a folk song does not signify an end to that song's development. Bajan folk songs such as "Murder in de Market" are still subjected to transformations and amendments. Since Gabby has recorded the 1985 folk composition "Emmerton," there have been several variations and developments of this song by the composer himself and other folk groups such as the Ellerslie folk chorale.[28] One shortcoming of Karpeles' conceptualization and categorization is that it does not place enough emphasis on the musical components of the folk song. But all in all, her insights are extremely useful.

What becomes evident to the researcher who goes through many sources in search of a generally accepted definition of folk music is the reality that there are probably as many definitions as there are writers on the subject. For example, in contrast to Karpeles' emphasis on oral transmission and the media of presentation, there are approaches like Courlander's which place more focus on musical form and structures:

> A great deal of American Negro music has been found to use the pentatonic scale . . . . Many Negro songs utilize other so-called "gapped" systems, such as the ordinary major scale lacking its fourth or its seventh—in other words, the pentatonic plus an additional note, either the major fourth or the major seventh. Other scales are the major with a flattened seventh, the minor with a raised sixth, the minor without the sixth, and the minor with a raised seventh . . . .[29]

There are still other approaches and philosophies which pay little attention to defining folk music but treat the folk song as a concept which exists in the minds of the community. This is the outlook of the English Folk Dance and Song Society and their magazine of the same name. In their first edition, the editorial does not set out or seek to outline a concept of the folk song.[30] In the final analysis, no one definition is likely to be universally acceptable. Alan Lomax's experiment with canto metrics in folk music begins with the perception that "there are powerful stylistic models shaping the majority of songs performed in large regions of the world."[31] But, as Lomax is careful to remind the reader, his all-embracing theory does not adequately deal with musical ideolects or dialects.[32]

Barbados has a tradition of folk songs which date back to the 1830s, and into the latter half of the present century. These songs deal with a variety of local subjects. Some songs retell socio-historical events while others are songs of socio-political commentary. Still others treat human themes such as love and infidelity while the rest are game songs. *Traditional Folk Songs of Barbados* provides the widest sample of Bajan folk songs from the nineteenth century to the early 1970s.

It is reasonable to assume that folk songs such as "Lick an' Lock-up Done Wid," "King Ja Ja," "Murder in de Market" and "Tonight is A Funny Day" comprised the repertoire of tuk bands in the past. The lively rhythms and simple melodic components would have made such songs popular with tuk bands, the Landship and audiences. These songs were kept alive and passed on from generation to generation by the tuk band. Their melodies were preserved either by the tuk band's lead singer in earlier times or, from the middle of the twentieth century, by the penny-whistle player. Ruk-A-Tuk International's interpretation of "Tuk Band Rhythm" provides an example of folk song performance over the decades.[33]

I do not pretend to possess a definitive theory of what constitutes a Caribbean folk song. However, since further analysis in this book is dependent on a working definition, I will make some general observations about the Caribbean folk song. For some commentators and audiences, what usually distinguishes Caribbean folk music from any other type of contemporary music is the component of time. A song such as "Conrad," written by Da'costa Allamby and performed in the 1960s by the Merrymen, is now conceivably folk, though at the time of composition it would have been calypso. But time is not and cannot be the sole determinant of what folk music is and is not since it is widely believed that present day artists continue to simultaneously compose both calypso and folk songs. In a debate which has proved inconclusive and exposes the high degree of sensitivity and subjectivity involved, one might tentatively posit a number of considerations of distinction.

First, let us consider the lyrics. As the genre folk suggests, they reflect a concern with collectiveness and community, usually among the average working class segment of the population. These lyrics engage and evoke some sort of national, local or cultural sentiment. Very rarely do they overstep the domain of country, but instead tend to be relevant and comprehensible to the average citizen. And when their focus is on some extra-territorial concern that is merely referential, it serves to highlight some truth or problem which is local. For example, Gabby's folk song "Lizzy" gets its title from Queen Elizabeth II,[34] but it is less about her and any royal visit and more about the local Bajan reaction. Its theme is obsequious neo-colonialism.

Comparatively, there is not much use and re-use of technical literary devices—such as irony or symbolism—which might obscure meaning and perception. In most cases the folk lyric readily identifies its subject and overtly explores its themes, making few excuses or secrets about its findings or conclusion. Contrary to popular conception, folk songs can be thematically diverse. The Barbadian folk songs' treatment of historical events include nationalism, aspects of everyday cultural life, political concerns, aging, death, dispossession and revolt.

In terms of its music the folk composition is characterized by employment of fewer musical instruments and instrumentalists than the other forms of Caribbean pop music. In the English-speaking Caribbean, folk music is often accompanied on performance occasions by the acoustic guitar or some other stringed instrument, and with a limited number of membranophones and percussive instruments. Musical composition, instruments and arrangement features are not nearly as important as rhythm, lyrics and meaning. Melody is often not a complex issue. There is repetition of melodic phrases and recurring chord structures and progressions, usually with much emphasis on the root, fourth and fifth positions within chord progressions.

The dangers of attempting to objectively and technically identify and label a song as "folk" are many and perilous. In the Caribbean, the surest way of identifying and labeling a piece is a reliance on the artist, in addition to testing a particular piece for some of the features touched on here.

Gabby has been voted top folk artist in Barbados on several occasions. This is only one category in which he has earned national awards. Apart from these types of rewards, Gabby insists that "the joys of performing to an appreciative audience" and approximating the status of social chronicler through his compositions is a much more fulfilling achievement. As a calypsonian, Gabby has performed with brass bands throughout the annual Crop Over Festival. For a period around 1988 he also appeared regularly with the now defunct combo called Caribbean Rhythms Band. As a folk performer he is both a singer and musician, accompanying himself on the guitar. What he lacks in the way of stage performance when he sits or stands with a guitar strapped over his shoulder, he makes up for by a greater emphasis on vocal flexibility and manipulation. On stage, Gabby the folk singer achieves a more intimate relationship, response and rapport with his audience than when he performs a calypso. A song like "Calypso," which extols the art form of kaiso as a powerful medium for social and political redress, is much more effective when performed in the folk song idiom than when performed or presented as a calypso. The folk-type performance is raw, fresh and sincere.

The dichotomy of this constant shifting by Gabby between idioms and its effect is played out by the 1991 Eddy Grant recording of the popular "West Indian Politician." The recording is given a folk-spiritual flavor. It lacks the richer ambiance of the eighteen piece Bajan festival band (considered one of the best backing bands at any calypso competition anywhere) which accompanied Gabby when he first performed the song in 1985 and won the calypso monarch title. Some have voiced the opinion that the production on Grant's Ice label is too folk or spiritual oriented, but these queries seem to come through a discomfort with hearing a musical co-text which transgresses what, for them, had become a fixed master-text. This attitude of disquiet and uneasiness ignores the dynamics which characterizes the structure and composition of such Afro-based music forms.

Conversely, one might relay the fault and inquiry to the other side. One might suggest that the Grant-Gabby experiments are too progressive and do not pursue the path that many local commentators would like to see them follow. (Subsequent segments of this book examine that other side of the artist-audience relationship in more detail.)

An important feature of folk-based artistic practices is their lingering value as cultural and historical documents. In this regard some compositions by Gabby are similar to those by Jeanette Layne-Clark, the oral-centered female writer of dramatic sketches. This similarity is most prominent in her socio-historical documentation found in "Okras in De Stew."

There is a category of Gabby's folk songs which treats everyday life occurrences and people, as opposed to those which focus on some special, significant incident. Within a Barbadian aesthetic these compositions share a number of similarities with some of Kamau Brathwaite's verse. That is, poems by Brathwaite which are about Barbados, in the Bajan voice, especially those found in *Mother Poem* and *Sun Poem*. Gabby's "Bajan Fisherman" conjures recollections of Brathwaite's fishermen sequence in segment thirteen of "Yellow Minnim." In *Sun Poem* we hear:

> In the great purple dawn the fishermen poured like priest to the shore. it was dark when they stopped, filling their cans with water that swished from the pipe like wind through a key hole: the tone getting deeper as the bucket filled up. then they moved on: walking in twos and in threes: tall black monks of the morning light wrapped in their cloaks because of the cold and their anti-salt-water coats; walking out of the night down the street ahead of the sun and under the leaves of the sea grape and cordia trees whose flowers were fast fading stars in the touching them softly light. and

before the houses awoke, before fathers opened windows and
doors, at the time when the first cocks crowed and the last dogs
barked at the passing ghost . . .[35]

In Gabby's "Bajan Fisherman," as in the above poem, the
mood created is one of reverence, relayed through the attitude of
ritual which *Sun Poem* creates by sequentially listing pre-dawn
duties. Gabby's reverent mood emanates from the repetition of
melodic tonal and lyrical motifs:

Sometimes I would sit on the de beach and I would talk
fisherman fisherman
Sometimes I would sit on de beach and I would
talk and talk (ad lib)

Sometimes I would sit on de beach and I would laugh (ad lib)
Fisherman (ad lib)
Bajan fishermen (ad lib) . . .[36]

This comparison of Brathwaite's and Gabby's song-poems
is not based on the scribal texts. In the case of the *Sun Poem*
extract, the comparison hinges on the oral and dramatic
performance as it was enacted during the 1986 stage one
dramatization of the poem. In the case of Gabby's song, it is
the voice and music which are largely responsible for creating
the song-poem's atmosphere. Whereas the lyrics of Gabby's
composition might appear thinner than Brathwaite's in print,
in performance the compositions' similarities are more easily
realized. The privileging of this type of inter-textual reading
seeks to mediate the distance and difference between texts not
frequently compared but which are related.

As with Brathwaite and Layne-Clark, Gabby's representation of
everyday folk life and ordinary people is less an exercise in polemics
and more an affirmation of the virtues of the folk and their type of
existence. It is an affirmation of their strength, resilience, thankful-
ness, humanness, wit, humor, insight and thrift.

The folk song "Bridgetown" not only documents and recreates the Saturday morning market days of "huckstering" in
Bridgetown's Cheapside Market, but is also a tribute to the
enterprise of the nation's women. In spite of legal moves to curb

their burgeoning sale and trade throughout and after the slave period, Bajan women have persisted. They continued to cultivate food and rear livestock. They were responsible for providing a considerable proportion of the island's food.

> . . . rearing and selling poultry, sheep, goats, hogs and their super-fluous allowance of corn and roots . . . induced the negroes to assume airs of consequence and put a value on themselves unknown amongst the slaves of former periods.[37]

The song-poem "Bridgetown" is a marvelously captioned artifact of twentieth century market day activity, which the performer enhances with his exaggerated [a:] syllables at the end of words such as *guavah* and *potatah* within the bridge-functioning segment of the song. The playing and employment of other stigmatized Bajan linguistic and socio-linguistic features, such as lengthening the [o] sound in *morning* and transforming it into something much closer to [a:], or interpreting *for* as [F^h], which enhances the effectiveness of the song-poem. But in addition to the hubbub of sellers and buyers, it is Gabby's mimic of the market "hollas" which is the song's single most effective and effervescent trait. He holds out the sellers' cries ". . . guavaaaaaaaaaaah . . ." sometimes the duration of two bars in a twelve beat bar, of a slow to slow-medium tempo composition.

> *Bridgetown early Suddaday morning*
> *yuh see de wuhmen how deh calling*
> *singing come fuh yuh breadfruit*
>
> *come fuh yuh corn come fuh de apple fresh as de morn*
> *come fuh bananah come fuh patatah*
> *come fuh de guavah, de guavah de guavah*
> *de guavahaaaaaaaaaaaaaaaaahaaaa . . .*
>
> *Bridgetown early Suddadah mornin*
> *yuh see de children how dey smilin singing . . .*
> *Dumplins in stew full up yuh bell wid lots o' fresh fruits*
> *come fuh yuh breadfruit come fuh yuh corn*
> *come fuh de apples fresh as de morn'*
> *come fuh bananah come fuh patatah*

come fuh yuh guavah yuh guavah yuh guavah
yuh guavahaaaaaaaaaaahaaaa . . .
Bridgetownnnnn eearrly Sataday morning
Maaaahnin, Maaahning Maaaahning
Maaaahning
Ladeydey langlangladeyleyang . . . (ad lib.)

Bridgetown early Saddaday morning
yuh see de peasants how de calling
singing come fuh yuh breadfruit
come fuh yuh corn come fuh de apple fresh as demorn'
come fuh banana come fuh patatah
come fuh yuh guava yuh guava yuh guava
Yuh guavaaaaaaaaaaaaaahaaa (ad lib).[38]

Like Brathwaite's persona in the poem "Francine" or his
mother motif in *Mother Poem* or his male principle in both Bajan-
centered poems in his second trilogy, the folk icons who figure in
Gabby's "John Brown" and "Gran' Ma Miriam" are victims of
society's cruelty and the socio-political system. Although they
represent the underprivileged and deprived, for Gabby the composer, impecuniosity is not the central attribute in these types of
artistic creations or their renderings. John Brown is the overworked and discarded peasant of the sugar industry who must
think of feeding his starving, dying children.

So John Brown went right back dey to de plantation
He took uh onion one small onion
so John Brown went right back dey to de plantation
He took uh onion one small onion
He took it because his son was crying
was starving was dying
That night a shotgun went a blasting
They shot him in his head and no time he was dead[39]

Gran Ma Miriam is the backbone of her society:

Gran Ma Miriam no woman could work like she
My Gran Ma Miriam no woman could work like she
Gran Ma Miriam no woman could work like she[40]

With a performer like Gabby such folk characters' voices are actually heard. The performer adapts the persona, impersonating the actions and taking on the voices of his subject. In many ways the folk singer is also a storyteller. Drama is often the essence of the folk poem. In "Needles an Pins" the proximity of storyteller and folk singer is evidenced by the suspicion (mine alone) that Gabby and Layne-Clark wrote collaboratively. The song presents a confrontation between two Bajan women who make one big "bacchanal" over the affection of a sweet man—one of the women's husband. The strength of Gabby's performance skills is apparent as he acts as an objective narrator who introduces the action with a series of candid explicatory gestures. He sings, "Johnny have two women, he wife an he girlfriend.... Hear now what goin' happen . . ."[41] On other occasions he becomes Johnny's wife. Here again he is Johnny's sweet woman who herself repeats the nagging half-menacing refrain to the wife, ". . . yuh can't have pins wid me. No needles an' pins wid me."[42] This giving and taking of insults makes for heightened drama, with Johnny's sweet woman having the upper hand over a less bombastic wife. With every chorus the performer dons the mask of mistress, assumes a high-pitched female voice but reworks its inflections, and supplements a fresh series of hurtful acts of cuckoldry to a brooding wife. As in many of the predictable endings of Layne-Clark's dramas like "Okras in the Stew," one anticipates that the wife will eventually retaliate to put an end to the nagging refrains of ". . . yuh can't have pins wid me. No needles an' pins wid me." In the end the wife does retaliate. But the irony (and indeed a success in terms of defeating audience expectations for the ending) resides in the composer's retention of the nagging refrain turning to how the wife ultimately causes the other woman to "take off like uh express train" as she inflicts blows. She concludes the matter with:

> . . . yuh can't have pins wid me
> Nuh needles an' pins wid me
> Uh don't care what yuh do Betty
> yuh mus still interfere wid me [43]

Few studies of Gabby's work trace the seeds of his potent social and political protest prior to the decade of the 1980s and fewer seem inclined to go beyond the rigidly conceived discipline of calypso. His defiant "Take Down Nelson" challenges the establishment to exorcise the ghost of the colonial lords symbolized by the statue of Horatio Nelson in Barbados' Trafalgar Square. This folk song insists on the urgency to "put up a Bajan man." His highly sensitive "Who Kill Pele," which comments on a widely rumored politically motivated murder, predated his 1980s spate of protest compositions in the calypso forum.

The history of post-Independence political life in Barbados is so polarized between its two political parties—Barbados Labour Party (BLP) and Democratic Labour Party (DLP)—that to criticize one is often interpreted as a ballot cast for the other. Gabby has not been spared his share of suspicion. Gabby has been a member of the DLP and ran on its ticket in 1994. Since his most consistent spate of social and political songs coincided with the ruling of the Tom Adams BLP Administration, the tradition of myopic political labeling has meant that the integrity of his art has come into question.

Political and other forms of patronage are by no means new to the practice of the performing arts. As an examination of the parent (African) tradition reveals, the artist's practice has always come under scrutiny—from the court poets to those affiliated with religious authority in some traditional West African societies. What this present interrogation represents is the ongoing linkage between the Caribbean tradition and its major parent influence of Africa. On another and perhaps more clear-cut level, it is a confirmation that no artist exists in isolation, but instead functions within society and is impacted on (or perceived to be) by its forces.

Comparatively few commentators seem to remember Gabby's 1976 folk song "Licks Like Fire." In it he sings about the political victory of the BLP and parodies the collapse of the DLP, who he condemns to being "gone fuh evah." This song met its parallel and reverse almost a decade afterwards with the BLP's defeat at the polls. The song "Backraise" recounts the events leading up to and throughout the 1986 post-election period when BLP leader

Mr. Bernard "Bree" St. John accuses the other party and populace of conniving to unseat and "backraising" his organization. As recorded texts both songs are similar in terms of political wit, satire and critique (of which Gabby is a clever exponent). There is no marked disparity in terms of vocal integrity, projection or other oral components of rendition other than the treatment of a more mature voice in "Backraise" and certainly the improved sound quality on this latter production afforded by the use of Grant's Blue Wave production facilities. First, "Licks Like Fire":

People start to frown [Wednesday] then they mouth drop down [Thursday]
When they hear de B.[L.P] was lickin de D. [L.P]
17 to 7 [Murdah] they said it couldn't happen [fire]
But de B's an' Tom [Adams] prove all uh dem wrong (uh tell you)

(chorus)
Licks like fire
De D.L.P gone for evuh
Licks like fire
De B.L.P now take ovuh
Licks like fire
Adams came out just like Ali
And brek up de D.L.P

They say no more tricks [no no] in '76 [no no]
And they had de whips [yes sir] yes to give dem de licks [yes sir]
Beat them in de north [district] in de south and west [district]
Even in de east [district] they tear off they vest

Licks like fire
Adams tell them bring de skipper
Licks like fire
I gon bite out all he livah
Licks like fire
And if he come up to St. Thomas
(look) I gon kick he all in he brass

Listen to this one [ah ah] cause this ain't no lie[ah ah]
When Bree win de seat [in Christ Church]

"Peanuts" start to cry [in Christ Church]
And one ministah [in Christ Church] watching on T.V [in Christ Church]
Couldn't take it no more get up to plee fall an break he knee

Licks like fire
Adams say you think I mekkin joke
Licks like fire
Uh changing de name of me airport
Licks like fire
From Seawell to great Sir Grantley
Licks like fire
(look) Who don't like it leave de country.[44]

Now compare with "Backraise":

Big budget speech got something special it
show de people de B's in trouble
They hang themselves lose them vehicle man
de people power making them tremble

They had we choak for ten long years we
moan an' groan blood sweat and tears
They hang themselves seal they own fate
that is how de 'dems' won de debate

And de only excuse that Bree could make
Dem people backraise we
Well he frighten cause he whole life at stake
Dem people backraise we
Well he lie he lie that is one excuse we can't buy
But he shoutin on radio and TV
Dem people backraise we
yes he shouting on radio and TV
Dem people backraise we
Backraise Backraise dem people backraise we: (4 times)

Well when Richie say he giving way 15,000 free from taxation that
*   cause confusion*

Well de critics say he statement need definition re-explanation for
  comprehension
So because of that Richie return and when he talk they start to burn
The manifesto of de B's cause Richie bring dem to they knees

When Vic Johnson bring out de corn beef I thought that was comic relief
Then I realize things still de same corn beef an' biscuit still stick in dey brain
And to cause dem even more sorrow man they introduce Errol Barrow
He play wid them like child wid toy an he mek Owen Arthur look like a boy.[45]

Gabby's most popular folk-oriented song is the socio-political "Emmerton" (the name of the artist's place of birth). The song bewails the uprooting of the peasantry in the name of socio-political development. Where the poet makes a promise that "I will never forgive you, cause looka wha yuh do wid my Emmerton," it is less a threat to a particular political party than it seeks to hold the political establishment accountable for a loss of contact with, and the discontinuation of, a particular way of life and tradition. This non-specific dialogue and attendant politics give "Emmerton" much appeal. This broad-based appeal is felt at some performance events when audiences of different affiliations demand to hear it performed. For performers like Gabby there can never be such a comfort as preparing a fixed package for a show. In alluding to the effect of audiences on some of his performances he reveals, "When ever uh get to a place . . . uh have ma programme set an' uh hear one voice in de back alone sayin' 'Emmerton' and then there is a chorus of voices 'yeah, Emmerton!!!'"[46]

It is at such moments that he smiles while looking over the audience with a guitar strapped around his slim frame. He winces, strokes his bristly beard, and smiles again in acquiescence. Then, as spontaneously as on that first time he composed this "anthem of the displaced," he is "so sad [his] fingers [walk] on the guitar to E minor"[47] a semitone lower than the 1985 Grant recording, for the comfort of a lower key and the greater flexibility for "emotional considerations" which it allows.[48] The greater impact of his live performance of "Emmerton" over the fixed recorded text rests on the raw untamed treatment which voice and guitar are able to create and transmit. Unlike the sustained intensity of the recorded version with its almost aggressive piano and ever haunting samples and voices of the synthesized flute and sequenced layers of synclavier strings, his live performance is even more sentimental in mood and tonal coloration. Compared to the recorded performance, his live performances are generally more dynamic—an effect which is created by his willful non-articulation of items, phrases and syllables. In the live performance we have the benefit of a physical expression—from facial squinching to closed water prone eyes and repeated nods of disgust and disbelief. These are played out to the accompaniment of willfully inconsistent rhythmic and metrical phrases, underlined by a crafty, effective and effectual manipulation of voice and fingers on and off the fret board.

you tell me tuh forget dat my gran mudah was born right there so
All right I say I shall go
yuh tell me tuh forget it is there I want my own children to grow
All right I say I shall go

(chorus)
But I hope yuh understan' how I feel 'bout Emmerton
My home land my home land my home land
An uh hope yuh know it's true that I will nevuh fuhgive you
Because looka looka wha' yuh do to my Emmerton

you tell me to fuhget dat yuh bring bulldozers an' push down de houses so
Alright I say I shall go
yuh tell me tuh fuhget yuh bring bulldozers an' push down de houses so
Alright I say I shall go

Yuh tell me tuh fuhget dat yuh uproot my people an' scattah them to an' fro
Alright I say I shall go
yuh tell me tuh fuhget dat yuh did them wrong things an' didn't let my
children know
Alright I say I shall go

yuh tell me tuh fuhget dat my gran muddah was born right there so
Alright I say I shall go

Alright I say I shall go
Alright I say I shall go
Alright I say I shall go
Alright I say I shall gooooo . . .[49]

NOTES

1 From "The Gabby Years." A docu-presentation aired on the Voice of Barbados (July 2, 1992).

2 Ibid.

3 Ibid.

4 Mark Williams was Barbados' most prominent show promoter within this era. He has spoken at length on a number of radio programs about the Barbadian music industry throughout the twentieth century. To hear Mark Williams, listen to "Strictly Bajan." CBC Radio (November 13, 1992).

5 Warner, Keith. *The Trinidad Calypso.* (London: Heinemann, 1982) 7–8.

6 Hill, Errol. *The Trinidad Carnival.* (Austin: University of Texas Press, 1972) 60-61.

7 Ibid.

8 Epstein, Dina. *Sinful Tunes and Spirituals.* (Urbana: University of Illinois Press, 1977).

9 Abrahams, Roger et al. *After Africa.* (New Haven: Yale University Press, 1983).

10 Rohlehr, Gordon. *Calypso and Society in Pre-Independence Trinidad.* (Port of Spain: H.E.M., 1990).

11 Cowley, John. "Music and Migration." Ph.D. dissertation (University of Warwick Press, 1992).

12 For more on the Joe and Johnny dance and its music, see Abrahams et al. *After Africa.* 313–315.

13 *The Trinidad Mirror.* (March 4, 1908) 14.

14 See note 11 above.

15 See note 11 above.

16 *The Weekly Guardian.* (February 17,1923) 10.

17 See note 10 above. 457.

18 "Too Late Corkie Too Late" as performed by Shilling.

19 Personal interview with Anthony "Gabby" Carter (July 1992).

20 Ibid.

21 "Heart Transplant." (1963).

22 Courlander, Harold. *Negro Folk Music U.S.A.* (New York: Columbia University Press, 1963) 15. For further debate in this area see Cecil Sharp's *English Folk Songs: Some Conclusions.* (London: Novella, 1916).

23 See Karpeles, Maud. *An Introduction to English Folk Song.* (Oxford: Oxford University Press, 1973) 1.

24 Ibid. 2.

25 Ibid.

26 Ibid.103–4. J.H. Nketia does not seem to agree with Karpeles' notion that a folk song cannot be recent. He points out that his collection of Ghanaian folk songs "are by no means sons of a forgotten past." *Folk Songs of Ghana.* (Legon: University of Ghana, 1963) 1.

27 See note 23 above. 104.

28 During folk night at the 1992 Crop Over Festival.

29 See note 22 above.

30 *English Dance and Song.* Vol. 1, No. 1 (English Folk Dance and Song Society, 1936).

31 Lomax, Alan. *Folk Song Style and Culture.* (New Brunswick: Transaction Books, 1968) 35.

32 Ibid. 34.

33 Listen to the folk song "Tuk band Rhythm" on *Traditional Tuk Band Music of Barbados* (Ruk-A-Tuk International, 1991).

34 The folk song "Lizzy" was titled after the royal visit of her majesty.

35 Brathwaite, Edward Kamau. *Sun Poem.* (Oxford: Oxford University Press, 1982) 25.

36 Carter, Anthony "Gabby." "Bajan Fisherman."

37 "The Report from a Select Committee of the House of Assembly appointed to inquire into the origin, causes and progress of the late Insurrection." (Barbados, 1818) 46.

38 Carter, Anthony "Gabby." "Bridgetown." *One in De Eye* (1985).

39 "John Brown."

40 "Gran Ma Miriam."

41 "Needles an Pins."

42 Ibid.

43 Ibid.

44 "Licks Like Fire."

45 "Backraise."

46 See note 19 above.

47 See note 19 above.

48 Carter, Anthony "Gabby." "Emmerton." *One in De Eye* (1985).

5 THE COMMERCIAL EDGE: SOCA AND AFTER

KAI-SOCA AND POLITICS

... but I cannot make a living from folk music, you know.[1] (Gabby)

As conscious as Gabby is of his commitment to what he sees as a tradition and folk-based idiom, he is equally cognizant of the artist's survival within the contemporary setting of an increasingly commercially-oriented marketplace. He has not given up on the idiom of folk music for there is much overlap between the genres of folk and calypso. Where folk is distinct and separate from calypso for some commentators, I have not been so rigid here. I contend that a significant number of Gabby's songs sung around the time of Barbados' seasonal Crop Over Festival (a festival marked by the proliferation of calypsos) are indeed folk-oriented as much as most of those songs we dealt with in the previous chapter. One might note his bona fide folk interpretation with the Ellerslie folk singers of the kaiso entitled "Culture" at folk night during the 1992 Crop Over Festival at Queen's Park. It is fallacious to assume that the Gabby-Grant affiliation has marked any total drifting away from the demands or tastes of a local folk patron. Gabby is at once the traditionalist and innovator—radical and maverick.

Egudu is constantly at pains to pinpoint satire, humor and wit as central to oral poetry in West Africa, and more specifically of the Igbo.[2] In the Caribbean context, Keith Warner sums up the dominant mood of the traditional calypso to be "one of humor," as the calypsonian is expected to come up with something unusual or witty to satisfy the listener.³ However, much contemporary calypso is agreed to be devoid of the volume of wit and satire of times past. It is said to lack the allegory of Spoiler, the humor of Lord Nelson, and the picong orientation of Charmer, Atilla and Lion.

It is a fact that the contemporary art form has not held firm to these features with a sustained level of persistence, or kept in the same vein as the "traditionalists" would have practiced, espoused and directed. Gabby is in no way a direct descendent or strict adherent of such traditional elements within the calypso, but as the social and commercial dictates have impacted and necessitated the reworking of such aspects, Gabby is as more akin to the West African style (Igbo, according to Egudu) than many other calypsonians.

Gabby is the type of songwriter who controls the emotions. He imparts a serious message but tickles his audience into the experience as he performs. When in 1985 it was discovered that the winner of a Miss Barbados beauty pageant was not a national, it was time for one of the region's sniping satirists to sound his voice. In a situation and context where this outcome was an embarrassment to an entire nation, some would have anticipated an all-out attack from the calypsonian—either a lampoon-filled dig at those responsible, or a direct, telling reprimand. Gabby opted for a mixture of both: satire. In his song he went from the straight-faced reported voice of each verse:

> *Barbados had a beauty competition*
> *Gals on television fighting to wear de crown*⁴

To the lampoon-filled call and response mode in each chorus:

> *Miss Barbados (chorus)*
> *Nevuh hear 'bout flying fish (soloist)*
> *Miss Barbados (chorus)*
> *Nevuh hear 'bout cou-cou⁵ dish (soloist)*
> *Miss Barbados (all)*
> *Don't know nuttin 'bout sea egg an' that's no lie*
> *Miss Barbados is as Bajan as apple pie (soloist)*⁶

In the second verse this pattern of tone sequencing is interrupted (through a quietly orchestrated though telling linguistic movement) by tampering with sound and rhythm patterns. Observe and listen:

Great publicity surrounded de occasion
Society welcome dis friendly invasion
All de talk was 'bout who look bes', yes!
Which girl has de mos' zes'
Who possess de nices' dress de beauty contes'
Had international judging . . .'

Here the songster is allowing sound and rhythm to work on his behalf. The sibilant sounds which ordinarily work well in describing such a sensuous setting are overworked for satiric effect within the four lines beginning in line three above. The effect is a series of quivering pulses of pseudo-absurd rhymes which fail to sustain the rhythm pulse employed in the first two lines and punctuated by the first couplet. Here the syllabic count can easily be lost to the quickening rhythm which seems to slip away seeking definition and punctuation . What should be the poised glide of a beauty queen becomes the exaggerated enthusiasm of a pretentious contestant who "possess" too much "zes'" to be true. Of course, no one believes the performer when he sings that the judging had "no hanky-pankying." The spirited "swinggggy" and rhythmic fast-medium accompaniment was no doubt conceived to contrast with the subject of regal poise.

It is a spirited musical arrangement, characteristic of the types of productions with which Grant was experimenting around the mid-1980s. Such compositions feature a riding laid-back bass with stated bars of sparse and occasional staccato pulses. These punctuations are usually played at the end of chorus and band chorus, playing around the root or tonic, supertonic, subdominant and dominant notes of the scale (a kind of beat-around), or as the chord progression requires. Such bass licks dominated the mix of many of Grant's recordings. But it is the percussion—the congas mainly—which are on top of this recorded arrangement. They weave with the characteristic pop-influenced down beat of a snare drum and synchronous hand clap on the second and fourth beats of each four-beat bar. The riffs of what must be live horns (or excellent samples thereof) are not predominant throughout the song (as they seldom are in any Grant arrangement). But they become active in each chorus by playing and responding at the end of each two-bar phrase and adding to the sense of drama between the soloist and chorus alluded to above.

Satire is employed in many other compositions ranging from concerns with medical policy ("Cadavers") to the follies and foibles of politics ("Backraise"). For satirists like Red Plastic Bag, satire is much more contrived. For Gabby, satire is hardly self-conscious and never a tool unto itself but is mostly a corollary of some other objective. For example, in the 1983 song "Cadavers" the calypsonian expresses the doubts of some sections of the society with regards to the proposed setting up of the Saint George's medical school in Barbados. The kaisonian seizes on the knowledge that the medical school will be engaged with research on the corpses of human beings. He engages in a series of exaggerated scenarios where members of the medical profession are portrayed as Dracula-type characters and Barbados is represented as being plagued with "duppies" (zombies). This composition is not an exercise in satire per se. It is concerned with voicing society's misgivings about the proposed introduction of the medical school. Satire becomes a method for conveying this opinion:

> *The injections that they giving*
> *Got people fitting in de casualty*
> *The prescriptions that they serving*
> *Got people wishing dey were dead already*
> *These bold-face murderers killing just for so*
> *Tell them Gabby say they must go*
>
> *(chorus)*
> *Look go to yuh butchuh he would sell yuh piece a cadava*
> *Look unduh tuh selluh dey hiding another cadava*
> *Uh tell yuh AAAaaaaaaaaaaaaHHHbhhh dem importing dracula.*
> *AAAaaaaaaaaaHHHHHHHHbhhhbhhhhhh dem importing dracula.*

(SkeLeToN . . . sKeleToN . . .

run run run run run from cadava

they want yuh MuddaHH for a cadava

they want yuh bruddaHH for a cadava . . .)

De excuses that they gi' we bout de duppy

Sound like real comedy

They say dey will bring Yankee money for this country

Well that is pure comedy

Who care bout Fort Knox when duppies can't deal de dough

De cemetery for all dem eye-soar[5]

Gabby's potential for demonstrating a shrewd sense of wit is best portrayed in the 1988 performance of "Who Gabby Tink He Is." In the song the performer becomes his own subject and object as he directs a series of society's misgivings about himself to himself and the audience. During a year in which there was much public dissatisfaction with what was generally seen as his arrogant demeanor, the artist sought to subvert these sentiments of hostility by reiterating and redirecting them to himself in public. The objective was a type of public apology, not a tearful admission of guilt, but a declaration that "maybe wunnah right." Here the skill of crafted construction and an effective rendition combine to produce a work whose success can be measured by the level of public participation which it has evoked. The refrain "Who Gabby tink he is" is the central slogan of the song. In performance it is shouted at the calypsonian by the audience, who become its chorus section of voices, although now, their intention is less belligerent and the whole affair is more of a negotiated act where the accused and his accusers perform together. Through this cleverly crafted and witty composition the artist was able to redeem and restore some of the public admiration which he had been in danger of losing.

Ah hear de talk ah hear de rumah

Gabby get too big fuh he boots

Ah hear de scandalous assassination of charactah (hear dem!)

Gabby get too big fuh he boots

From de time he come wid "Jack" he feel he was big like Goliath

Strong like Samson baadh like ah lion
He refuse to participate in we local competition
Went Trinidad and come in numbah sevun
(you should hear dem!)

(chorus)
Who Gabby tink he is (audience)
That he could refuse to sing fuh we to go Jamaica wid Byron Lee (Gabby)
Who Gabby tink he is (audience)

Evuh time he keep uh little show he gotta invite Dr. Sparrow
Tell him I say we put him dey to reign
And we got de powah to pull he back down again
(you should hear dem!)
Tell him I say dese tings he have to regret
And uh sorry dat Lovindeer didn't pop off he neck
(you should hear dem)
Who Gabby tink he is (wha dey all say)
Who Gabby tink he is
Who Gabby tink—Ah woman say
I waiting to cuss he stink cause
Who Gabby tink he is . . .

Ah hear he went on Television (you should see him)
Acking like he own de TV
An he cuss real bad on de radio station (hey)
I could see he is a bully (look!)
He playing 'higher-up an bettah off on de board of tourism
Fuhgettin dat he come from de dungeon in Emmerton
Where de lice, chinks an shigoas use to be his companion
Time tuh teach dah man a lesson
(you should hear dem)

I hear he rob Grynner and all dem Calypsonians
That is why he done wid de tent
I hear he cuss and fuss and fight wid all dem musicians
(believe me), he refuse to pay them a cent
He have to compromise an' cut down to size

He wife run and left he
She now living easy in New York city
All he got now is nuff bad-looking bony stab-out children
time to teach dat man a lesson[9]

In songs such as "Know No," "Faces" and "Bow Wow Wow!" Gabby has captured much of the sheer, light-heartedness and humor which is lamented to be lacking in the contemporary calypso. A composition such as "Bow Wow Wow!" for instance, though written for and performed by calypsonian Carew, is effectively humorous and simple enough that it captured a great deal of public attention throughout much of 1989 with its barking refrain of:

Bow wow wow
Bow wow wow
Bow wow wow
Put down my dog chow[10]

The composition recounts the physical and verbal encounter between a dog and a thief who breaks in and does the unpardonable—attempts to steal some dog chow. The comic flavoring of the composition is informed by employing allegorical fantasy. The owner is the song's narrator but the dog puts forth its own case quite well in each chorus, and in an occasional line in the verses. Here are a few scenes from the dog's adventure:

Bow wow wow
Bow wow wow
Bow wow wow
Put down my dog chow

I had a dog a big fat dog
He eat like a hog and bark like a frog
One night a tief brek in to my place
You should see my dog all over de place

Bow wow wow
Bow wow wow
Bow wow wow
Put down my dog chow
De man tek a jump and try to run away
My dog mek a snap and bite he pun he ear/tail
You could da tek de fridge video or TV
But you cross de wrong bridge and tek my food from me
De man tell de dog spare me for goodness sake
I had no right in hey I begging for a break
De dog say try your best this is de seas' of fleas
Just freeze an' do not sneeze I giving you rabies[11]

Gabby is arguably one of the region's few remaining stalwarts in the performance of picong. He credits his unique ability to create extemporaneously for much of his success on stage. There can never be such a thing as the fixed performance for an artist of such an inclination. The possession of the skill of improvisation often translates into a sense of expectation and anxiety within audiences, who are quite aware of this performance technique, and who demand an exhibition of such skill in each performance. The July 1990 attempted coup in Trinidad and Tobago only preceded the national calypso finals of Barbados by hours. Yet on that very night of competition the performer Gabby took a great risk in altering his lyrical text. He rendered a new verse in his calypso about Bajan-Trini confrontation "Flyin' Fish Diplomacy." This was performed much to the delight of a knowledgeable audience who had recognized its distinctness from, say, previous renditions and from the recorded version.

It is this picong element with which Gabby dabbles on occasion in his numerous references in songs to himself and other exponents at home and throughout the region. This is an attempt to elicit some sort of response and, hence, extend the tradition of "the calypso war" (of which Atilla and Lion are perhaps this century's best known exponents). In a song like "De List," for example, which is about a reputed list of male sexual partners formulated by a dying "young fellah," calypsonians such as Arrow and Sparrow find themselves being short-listed, more through Gabby's own playfulness than in any serious sense. Significantly, a year after this composition there was a response, not by Arrow of Montserrat, but by King Arrow of St. Maarten in his calypso "Take My Name Off De List." Although such an anti-homosexual song might be in poor taste in other cultures (like Europe), it was a relatively popular song in the Caribbean wherever it was played. This Caribbean attitude of revulsion towards homosexuality is based on a religious concept which sees homosexuality as sin. The effect of Gabby's addition of other names in the final chorus next to those which were really rumored to have been on the list, has the effect of steeping his song in rumor, hence making him less culpable. The public is sure that he wants to highlight some of the "big names popular names" who "mek love to de boy to cool down he burning flames"—and he does. But through extending the list he creates a defense (in numbers):

Uh young fellah die at de hospital an' it causin big bacchanal

Before de young fellah pass away he say wid who an' who he did play

Big names popular names was involve wid he playin some funny game

So now de women he dey had ain't taking no risk

They insist de hospital show dem de names pun de list

(look) Trevor name pon de list

And Dennis name pon de list

Lindon name pon de list and Tony name pon de list

Well what is dis list oh what is dis list dat cuttin like razor blades

This is de list wid de fellah dat got de aids

This is de list

This is de list dis is de list wid de fellahs dat got de aids

This is de list

This is de list dis is de list wid de fellahs dat got de aids

Nurse Bagalow say look boy I don't know ah hear

Gabby an' Plastic Bag there also

Grynner Pompey Destroyer Director de only name ain't there is Cubbah

Big names popular names mek love to de boy to cool down he burnin' flames

All de calypsonians bout hey too fast and too wild

'Cause if they don't catch de aids they bound to end up wid child

(And then she tell ma) Sparrow name pon de list and Arrow name pon de list
Explainer name pon de list Bruddah Mudada name pon' de list
Dis is de list . . .

Nurse Bagalow say what frightenin' me I went wid one o' dem recently
Dis fellah real macho wid nice body I didn't know he was a she-she'
Big names popular names know they love de men and still playin round de dames
Boy look this is what I call a real knock-out blow
So uh beg yuh all yuh do don't let Lick 'mout Lou know[12]

Gabby is best known for his political songs of protest. These go back to the 1960s and 1970s, but it is the early 1980s that proves him a powerful voice throughout the region.

The early 1980s was a critical stage in the development of political life in the Caribbean. The rising sense of confrontation between the capitalist and socialist world was being played out within the politics of local life throughout the region. The socialist revolution of Maurice Bishop in Grenada had sparked a war of words between Bishop and the prime minister of Barbados, Tom Adams. The question of the need to "restore democracy" in Guyana was heavily on the minds of Caricom leaders, and rumors of several impending mercenary takeovers in St. Vincent and Barbados all added to the precarious political climate of the time. Within a local context, the perceived deepening of economic hardships and loss of national sovereignty (symbolized by the coming of the International Monetary Fund (IMF) and increased military spending) were giving rise to a sentiment of opposition towards these dynamics.

Calypsos such as the defiant "Jack" (1982), which championed the local citizen's right of access to all beaches, was construed by the political leaders as negative tourism promotion for the island. But for the average citizen (and as far as on the continent of Africa) it was a firm rebuke to the mendacious temperament which was being implanted through the "tourist is always right" slogan. In one verse Gabby reminds the administrators:

My navel string buried right here
But a touris' one could be anywhere "[13]

In the following years Gabby's works would be the object of much censorship, both from the government-owned station and other media establishments. But the power, wisdom and prophesy of their message translated into a phenomenal public response—one which has remained unequaled in the contemporary Barbadian calypso context. Hard-hitting songs such as "MR. T" (MR. Tom Adams) and "Stinging Bees" (referring also to the BLP administration), though not performed by Gabby, were composed and written by him for his long-time friend and fellow calypsonian, Grynner. These, along with "Cadavers" and "Boots" and "One Day Comin' Soon," constitute a string of massive hits.

An interesting observation to be made is that all of the above songs are up-tempo in treatment and extremely danceable. This served to betray the feeling about the calypso that a serious message could and should only be imparted through the slow and labored rhythm, and that the up-tempo variety was purely "wine and wuk-up" (gyration of the hips). These compositions called for an analysis of the relationship between the lyric and other compositional features. The Bajan calypso is in many ways a contemporary innovator in this regard; it confirms the possibility of a successful merging of commercial sound with hard-hitting lyrics. Sparrow himself remarked on the success with which a sizable number of Bajan kaisos have been internalized, reworked and explore the dynamics of the art form in this way. Ice Records has pioneered this trend in Caribbean music.

"Boots" is Gabby's most commercially successful composition. It has sold (on disco 45's) comparatively well throughout the region, but the practice of illegal music reproduction and sale "pirating" has taken its toll on what could have been an even more financially successful recorded product. The artist laments how anything in the vicinity of 75 thousand copies might have been distributed illegally within the region's biggest island market alone—Jamaica. Whereas there should be considerable satisfaction in knowing his compositions had been in such great demand throughout the region, Gabby is quick to retort that this is his job—the profession of composing, performing and recording— and though all exposure is good the reality is that the artist must live and provide for his family—in Gabby's case for his "nuff…bony stab-out[14] children."[15]

In addition to his commercial successes throughout the region and among Afro-Caribbean populations in the American and European metropoles, the lyrics to his song "Boots," which deals with the increased proliferation of the military within the region in the early to mid-1980s, were featured in *Time* (April 5, 1985). The success of "Boots" stems from the appropriate timing of its composition, its effective lyrical and musical interpretation, and the performer's delivery, such as when he dons military garb and grabs a microphone.

Left right left right to de Government boots de government boots
Left right left right to de Government boots de government boots
Left right left right to de Government boots de government boots
Left right left right to de Government boots de government boots
Is it necessary to have so many soldiers in this small country
Noooo Nooo Noo Nooooo
Is it necessary to shine soldier boots wid taxpayers' money
Noooo Nooo Noo Nooooo
Well don't tell me tell Tommy he put them in St. Lucy
Unemployment high an' de treasury low so he buying boots to cover soldier toe

(chorus)
(I see them)
Boots boots Boots an' Mo, boots
On de feet o' young trigger happy recruits
(I see them)
Boots Boots Boots an' mo' boots
Marching threatening army troops
Tell Tom I say that wouldn't do he go to see 'bout me and you
An' most of all our lil' children
An' stop them soldiers from marching
Left right left right to de government boots de government boots

Was it necessary to hire dem soldier jokers to out a fire
Noooo Nooo Noo Nooooo
Was it right to give dem weapons they claim was unloaded to shoot Vincentians
Noooo Nooo Noo Nooooo
Well don't tell me tell Tom man he send them to Vincy land
Gun in they hand making a stand to quell a nonexistant rebellyan

Can we afford to feed that army while so many children naked and hungry
Noooo Nooo Noo Nooooo
Can we afford to remain passive while that soldier army growing so massive
Noooo Nooo Noo Nooooo
Well don't tell me mash Tommy heels he giving dem four square meals
Some o' dem so fat they could hardly run but they shooting bullseye wid
    automatic gun[16]

An artist like Gabby seems to relish the kinds of compositions
which allow and require the use of the mask or persona. His
experience in the theater is no doubt the source of such an
attitude. Gabby's stage presence can rise to be on par with other
features that are considered to be more significant within the
calypso. In some respects, his impersonations (e.g., in "Needles
an' Pins" and "Hit it") are more than impersonations. As with
some West African performers and definitely for Gabby, the
donning of a mask can be more than a psychological disguise
(which is its meaning for Western civilization). It gives birth to
a living and effectual instrument and is employed as ". . . a means
of participating in the many-sided life in the universe, creating
new realities beyond the merely human ones.[17]

In the performance of "Hit It," a double entente composition
about playing cricket with Jill, the refrains of "Hit it in de covah,
Hit it in mid-wicket" are met with firm, authentic kinesthetics
and antics which demonstrate the artist's awareness of the sport
and its field placings. But he also knows the technically correct
methods of romantic play, or he knows them too well, for
subsequent to a 1983 showing of one of his performances of "Hit
It" there was a barrage of complaints made on one of the nation's
call-in programs castigating the performer's behavior as "lewd."
Perhaps this had more to do with the apparent incongruity of the

test cricket player correctly attired for sport and engaging in frequent moments of slightly salacious gyrations. Or maybe the uproar was a manifestation of ignorance on the part of some onlookers. It is semiotician Umberto Eco who makes the point in *Carnival!* that, "When an unexpected and unauthorized carnivalization suddenly occurs in 'real' everyday life it is interpreted as revolution.[18] Perhaps this has been the case with Gabby—not with one composition only but with most of his early and mid 1980s calypsos—since for the first time these and the Bajan calypso were being played outside of the allocated season of the Crop Over Festival, and outside the confines of Barbados. Such is a possible explanation for the wave of political and social furor which surrounded his ground-breaking works.

The ensuing years brought with them a less militant approach to issues of political concern. Many people have interpreted this as the artist succumbing to political patronage since the coming to power of the DLP administration. Few commentators have remarked on his continuing militant stand on social issues. Issues such as the drug trade ("Rambo-Gabbo is Rambo"), the stuffed-under-the-carpet race and color complex in Barbados ("Mulatto"), the stagnation of political life even after the forming of a third political party—the National Democratic Party ("Windforce"), and the hypocrisy of the cricketing and political establishments vis-a-vis their hurried embracing of cricketers from what was still "de same South Africa" ("Rebels"). The kaiso "Send a Answer Fuh We" is arguably his most daring political statement on the state of affairs in Barbados in 1993:

Sometime I sit and I get so depressed

I can't express or lift off my chest

This burdensome stress that grinds my whole life in a mess, oh yes!

I mean de pain de proverbial rain

That falls on my brain time and time again

How can I explain it is too much strain

And I see it coming again

I would like to talk about de taxation

That causing starvation yes malnutrition in this nation

My friends I would like to say we in trouble economically
but I too frighten to tell it to anybody.

So I singing oh Lord send a answer fuh we.
Politicians fool we de priest fool we
Police and military leave we in a jeopardy
Oh Lord send a answer fuh we.

Crime on de increase we living like beast
How can it cease when police shoot police
in de station we consolation is investigation
and them soldiers taking drugs as well
as de government vans and start to sell
to you you and me any body
who would pay them enough money
but I would like to say de bishhop of Drexel
criticizing de government while his church
going down in hell
My friends I would like to say that Gatherer and he destroying christianity
and he may soon have to beg
Gather have mercy on he

If you don't notice de situation
something wrong with your observation
you can't help but see de mass corruption that surrounding we
who work so hard to make this our land
a shining beacon a utopian
example to follow turn to sorrow
with no hope for tomorrow
but I would like to say that Tudor de MP
prove decisively that he is not a Johnny come lately
I would like to say Harold Blackman and he
Them two don't fear Sandi
But I too frightened to tell it to anybody.[19]

Within this composition the persona assumes the voice of an apprehensive spokesman, one who is forced to speak out on account of the blatant increase in social and political misdeeds. It is significant that Gabby should frame this narrative with this type of tonal attitude. By doing this he plays upon what he knows is his audience's perception of his compromising relationship with the DLP administration. Thus, the persona and Gabby become synonymous within the song. The persona is heard expressing Gabby's dilemma—he is "too frighten to tell it to anybody."

Part of the intrigue of this song has to do with the ways in which it interacts within its own discursive space. By this I am referring to the way in which the song and persona negotiate the act of publicly critiquing a position for which its composer has been and continues to be a supporter.

The context and objective of composing this song are similar to those surrounding "Who Gabby Tink He Is." This earlier song identifies Gabby as its subject as a means of counteracting the public's growing disaffection towards him. "Send a Answer Fuh We" attempts to reaffirm to the public eye his commitment to political protest. The repetition of "I would like to say . . ." proves to be ironic in that the persona does actually say what he considers to be the unmentionable.

This song is admittedly different from commentaries such as "Boots" and "One Day Comin Soon." Whereas those songs present a consistent criticism of an opposing factor, "Send a Answer Fuh We" criticizes a number of social institutions (i.e., government, church, police and soldiers). It points to the general decay of a nation. Although it might be suggested that it does not attain the same level of intensive criticism achieved in the other two songs, the point is no less critical. What must be conceded is that this song's use of a labored tempo means it achieves a different effect than the two former compositions which are up-tempo in rhythm; whereas they are insistent and defiant, this one is supplicatory and reformative.

Gabby has been prophetic in some regards, for example in condemning the televangelist Jimmy Swaggart as:

Dis vindictive and wicked man
Walkin' bout wid Bible in hand
Promising you de promise land
Winning you into his money plan[20]

And chiding Bajans for:

Sending money to he in America
Meanwhile dem got relatives here who badly suffer
Dey won't give them a bloody cent
To buy food or even pay rent
Telling them that they must repent
And stay holy all through de lent.[21]

He compares Swaggart to Praise The Lord (PTL) Ministries, James Falwell, and Jim Baker. Months subsequent to the release of this recording the Swaggart scandal would break. Although his song "Illegal Tender" does not focus on the value of the Bajan currency per se, its release predated the widespread rumors of an impending devaluation of the Barbados currency by almost a year.

The attempts at achieving greater commercial success brought Gabby to compose a number of romantic ballads using the calypso idiom. Gabby is not the special purpose poet as Finnegan described the West African counterpart. He is akin to the freelance specialist:

... a poet who moves from place to place according to where he can find a wealthy patron or audience prepared to reward him ... but even if he spends a certain amount of time at the courts he does not hold an official and exclusive position[22]

The dynamics of his practice have facilitated a series of experiments with the lyrics and music of his compositions, especially in the latter half of the 1980s. The repercussions have been many; his native patrons and others often revert to the early and mid-1980s as his true glory days. A sizable percentage of his audience seemed unsure about his songs and commented on his 1992 crossover song "Rock" as "sounding strange" and "dat ain't nuh calypso song Gabby singin."

Between 1986 and 1988 Gabby attempted a number of calypsos employing an economy of words and clarity of imagery and meaning (a sort of Imagism?) in an attempt to reach further abroad. No one has gauged the total outcome of the experiment which has produced works such as "Jimmy Swaggart" and "Rambo" to name but two compositions. What is certain is that Gabby is constantly shaping his craft. It is this kind of outlook and approach which he offers to young artists and advises them to "chisel your talent."[23]

The number of love and romance ballads in the calypso have been coming a bit quicker for this artist since 1985. The concomitant experimentation with various rhythms and fusions have given rise to creating a number of character nationalities. In the calypso "Gisela," Gisela hails from Panama. In the composition "Puerto Rico," the San Juan "chick" is "every bit a beauty" and he encounters her in the glamour of the big city—New York (the perfect setting for the sale of his composition). This market-oriented tool has led Gabby to recording a ballad written by a British associate, the late Norman Beaton (of the television comedy "The Desmonds") in which the persona pleads with his Melvina to "come on back." "Only Cheating" is another composition in this mold: A cuckolded husband and a neglected wife advise solace in each other's loneliness. Such ballads are replete with repetition, especially in the chorus, and revolve around catchy medium-tempo musical arrangements and a romantically colored vocal rendition.

"Guilty" is arguably a more radical departure in terms of the composition of kaiso's musical text. This song borrows and utilizes influences from the reggae aesthetic. Most noticeable is its employment of the 1970s downbeat of the snare and kick drum. Its vocal rendition is akin to that of the pop balladeer. Gabby creates its effect through the use of a higher tonal voice coloration. What locates this musical text within the kaiso genre is its deliberately persistent calypso guitar strum. The guitar track is played against the heavier presence of drum and bass. Drum and bass punctuation might be said to rule the mix, but at its heart (in the mid and high-mid range frequency response spectrum) it is the treatment of the guitar's strum which mediates the apparent distance between this musical text and the tradition and style of the calypso. But its retention of the kaiso elements signifies the prohibitive force which still imposes a set form on kai-soca, one which ensures that kaiso does not go the way of the region's reggae or dancehall.

"Rose," another example of this hybrid model, holds even fewer connections to calypso. This recording signals what could be the redefining of the kai-soca idiom: its interaction and interface with other Caribbean and international forms. For the calypso experts, most of whom monitor and gauge the worth of artists by their political commentary, criticism of the establishment, and ability to write a "competition song," Gabby of the late and post-1980s period is perceived as moving further and further away from the tradition. Gabby clearly has a more liberal perception of what the artist should be. Although many commentators have criticized his philosophy, fewer individuals seem to be critical of the standard of presentation of his work. This artist has commented on many spheres of Bajan, Caribbean and human life. He has also ignored what has been the prescribed formula for composing and presenting kai-soca.

His crossover song "Rock" epitomizes some of the radical breaks from the tenets of kaiso which Ice Records is spearheading. This song is a kaiso-rap-fusion in which Gabby "doubles up" in the performance. As a lyrical text it fits the formulaic frame of the soca narrative as it extols the imperative of "rock[ing] dis place tonight." Its strength as a recorded performance text relies partly on Gabby's lively interpretation and transference of the lyrics of party into the mood of total chaos.

This composition epitomizes a phase of Ice sound represented by other sound texts like the earlier recording of "Roberta Flack." This sub-genre in Ice sound still placed emphasis on the bass, in terms of its place within the soundscape and sound level of the mix, but the bass textures became rounder. It is still synthesized but less self-attracting and more authentic in sound than what we hear in other recordings like "Puerto Rico" (a late 1980s recording).

I believe that the post-1980s richer, more ambient bass textures and Grant's tendency to strip the compositions to their percussive constituents signal the movement towards the most recent Ice phenomenon: *ringbang*.

Grant and Ice had been experimenting with a similar style of music much earlier in Bajan music. In a song like "Jack" (which employs the tuk drum) there is one of the earliest references to what in ten years would become ringbang. Were the 1982 version to be remixed with the drum and bass track foregrounded, then you would hear ringbang (or something close to it). Grant's own experiments with drums in other songs, such as "De List," "Illegal Tender," "Roberta Flack," "Rambo," "Ms. Barbados," "Puerto Rico" and "Arm de Police," all signal earlier explorations. These types of recorded texts are the forerunners of the phenomenon called ringbang.

RINGBANG AS CULTURAL APPROPRIATION?

In speaking of post-soca texts, it is possible to identify a number of developments within soca itself. For example, this section could be a focus on ragga soca or any other hybrid of soca. It could also be a segment which offers a comprehensive analysis and critique of the interface between soca and tuk.

The fact that this book on Barbadian music devotes a section to ringbang should not be interpreted as a political act on my part to co-opt this phenomenon as exclusively Bajan. Rather, its inclusion within this book is legitimate on a number of grounds. The majority of ringbang songs up to this point are performed by Barbadian artists. Barbados is the present "home base" of ringbang's creator, Eddy Grant; it is from here that he fashions the art form for regional and global dissemination. Throughout this book I have been exploring the relationship between Gabby as artist and Grant as producer and businessman. This section on ringbang expands on that debate and situates that dynamic within the more recent phase of its development. We have been very concerned with the demands of market forces and the impact of commercial and international imperatives on the music of artists like Gabby. Whereas we have traced the roots of Gabby's music to folk and examined its developments through calypso, soca and other fusions (and infusions) of pop, ringbang may be yet another genre in which he and artists like himself began to experiment. Ringbang refers more to a style of interpreting a song than to an actual music form itself. This style features the playing of the drums and a rhythmic emphasis up front.

In response to the question, "What is ringbang?" Eddy Grant describes it as a "constantly evolving thing" in which drums are most important. He suggests that ringbang places emphasis on rhythm—a natural phenomenon in life.

> You know, people talk about melody, but there can be no melody without rhythm. Rhythm is the most natural thing in the world. Listen to the wind—it has rhythm. The way we speak, there is rhythm to that. The way you drive your car, you have to do that with a certain flow, rhythm. You can't escape it. And that is what ringbang is all about.[24]

His insistence on ringbang going "across any border, interpreting the classics in our way" locates a subversive strategy in which ringbang will be engaged. Perhaps Grant's insight offers an indication of the kinds of songs and productions on which he intends to concentrate in popularizing ringbang. This is one dimension in which ringbang may to be divergent from calypso and soca. In orientation and practice, these two genres are insistent on the creation and production of culture-specific texts. Calypso and soca have never placed great emphasis on performing cover versions of cross-cultural texts. Conversely (and especially in the case of calypso), they lay stress on the original composition as an integral process for helping to define and sustain their particular tradition. I am not in any way suggesting that kaiso or soca do not throw up covers of international or other songs. Someone like Rudy Grant, the brother of Eddy Grant, has recorded numerous pop standards within the kaiso idiom. The mighty Sparrow and Baron have done covers as well. And some other artists have attempted to recontextualize pop songs by playing their lyrics on to the rhythms of calypso and soca. However, kaiso has not thrived on this type of intertextual practice—a method which Grant suggests as being vital to the performative freedom of ringbang.

Having gained the rights to a huge catalog of old calypsos, Grant's drive to re-record and distribute some classics could bring the application of ringbang to some of these songs. Thus far, Grant's drive to redefine the classics is marked by the production of Stalin's rendition of Bob Dylan's "I Shall Be Released." Also of note is the work Ice has been doing with the legend Roaring Lion. Based on what little has been communicated about ringbang, it is evident that the rhythm is attempting to free up the kai-soca art forms and formats by emphasizing less restrictive modes of creating. My reference to this phenomenon as a rhythm is itself restricting, in that ringbang seeks to be defined as more than a rhythm. Grant suggests that "it is the thing that keeps a baby quiet . . . it is what a mother sings to her baby. . . . It is what puts your soul at ease." Eddy Grant further explains that it is "a whole philosophy." As part of this philosophy he envisions "people wearing ringbang shirts, hats, ringbang for parties, ringbang for graduations . . . a lifestyle."

Is it partly because of this outward looking orientation in ringbang that I am seeing greater similarities therein with reggae, and more particularly with dancehall. Throughout its development reggae has always been less restricting to its artists than calypso. Reggae has been translated into an international consciousness largely because of its initial grounding in a philosophy which also sought to communicate to a larger audience. I am not saying that rasta per se has catapulted reggae and dancehall into the international scene and market, but I suggest that reggae's diasporic engagement and exploration is partly responsible for its perpetuation and major international appeal. Rasta became the metonymy for the dialectic binarism of "sufferation" and liberation. Reggae was able to engage a politics which had sustained international appeal. Reggae has always perpetuated its expansion through tolerance of its own and other creative dimensions of fusion. These dimensions have been afforded freer practice and greater acceptance than corresponding movements within calypso.

As a co-text of calypso, ringbang seems to place emphasis on expanding its own base in the manner of dancehall (by crossing other boundaries) as a means of expanding its influence. Although it has been suggested that ringbang is like soca in purpose (in that it attempts to free up calypso to the wider possibilities of its development), I tend to situate ringbang as representing a more radical departure. One should take note of Viking Thundah's chanting to the rhythm of Gabby's "Dr Cassandra" in his "De Stamina." The chanting mode is also employed in other ringbang texts. This practice of riding a rhythm is not a common practice in soca. Perhaps this is the point where dancehall and soca meet. Apart from the slogan "soca is the soul of the calypso," soca has never persistently expressed any wider socio-ideological or political imperative. Ringbang offers itself as a global phenomenon; one which translates into a set of practices which have application to and implications for different ways of life. Like the dancehall phenomenon, ringbang promises to thrive on international engagement.

Grant's vision of ringbang shirts, hats and other items places this phenomenon in the domain of the commodity form. It is this tendency—this market-oriented "universal drive"—which clearly situates ringbang as closer to reggae and dancehall than to calypso, though the central ideology at the base of ringbang (as stated by Grant) is not a material imperative. Ringbang assumes a focus for engaging a national, regional and international audience. To reflect on soca's rise in the late 1970s and early 1980s is to remark on the energies and efforts which were expended in attempting to validate or negate its claims to legitimacy. A sizable number of the misgivings expressed about soca tended to interrogate its claimed relationship with calypso. Some early rejections by the likes of Sparrow were based on the belief that calypso was an entity which needed no co-text to sustain its tradition. In the early days and years subsequent to its birth, soca was plagued by this type of contention. It had to delay any drive towards international dissemination on account of an initial attempt to validate its status in relation to calypso. I suggest that the practice and development of soca was affected by the calypso proper. Within the 1970s and 1980s, soca maintained sub-textual status in relation to the master text of calypso. It was only in the late 1980s, that it began to approach co-textual status in relation to calypso. Worldwide, calypso is still a more popular term than soca in respect of name recognition, and this in spite of soca's commercial orientation, practice and thrust. But this point should not distort the reality that soca sells better than calypso in the market place.

At present, from all indications, ringbang is making some impact on a younger audience. Because of this phenomenon's outlook it begins to connect with the lifestyles, language and interests of younger people. The early performers of ringbang are a mixture of experienced artists, young acts, and a more radical faction of socio-political commentators. There is every indication that this music will see an increasing focus placed on younger performers. The greatest impact has thus far been made by *Fire in the Wave* (CD) and *Ringbang Rebel Dance* (CD), and (outside of Barbados) by Super Blue's *String of Trinidad Carnival Hits Since 1995*.

Based on what has been released so far, the lyrics of this new style are similar to those which we associate with soca and with party. If *Fire in the Wave* can be used to gauge the lyrical content which will characterize ringbang, then the emphasis is squarely on fete, with little interest in socio-political commentary.

When one considers that the lyrical content of Afro-Caribbean radical Adisa Andwele in "Jump in De Ringbang Tide" and "Bring It Up" is devoid of substantial reference to social concerns, then I think we begin to understand the kinds of imperatives which this phenomenon imposes at the present.

Jump up feel de vibe
Jump up feel de vibe
Jump up feel de vibe
You gotta jump in de ringbang tide.

Yuh feeling down yuh feeling wrong
yuh gotta get up of o' de ground
yuh feeling stress yuh got to rest
Time to get up and be de best
Time to get up and raise yuh hand
Time to get up and join a band
Time to get up and take a stance
Time to jump to the ringbang dance.
Get out a bed don't play yuh dead
Yuh got to trod and lift up instead

Yuh got to fete yuh got to get
Time to party tuh yuh soaking wet
Time to jump up and raise yuh hand
Time to jump up and join a band
Time to jump up and take a stance
Time to jump to de ringbang dance.

It's time to chant it's time to scant
Time to wassy with de ringbang dance
Get out de bind yuh soul must shine
Let go now for de rhythm is fine
Time to jump up and raise yuh hand
Time to jump up and join a band
Time to jump up and take a stance
Time to jump to de ringbang dance.

Feel de vibe in your head let de music come alive
right now right now
Feel de vibe in you head let de music come alive
right now right now

Get out de door don't be a bore
for de sleep you got to ignore
Do not jive but come alive
Time to sail pun de ringbang tide
Time to jump up and raise yuh hand
Time to jump up and join a band
Time to jump up and take a stance
Time to jump to de ringbang tide.[25]

Prior to his appearance on the Ice label, Adisa had been experimenting with a number of rhythms. He had been consistently employing them to accompany his lyrics of African, Black and Caribbean empowerment. He has attempted soca fusions in songs like "Light a Candle" (in which he decried the ills of the world against its own children) with conviction, and in an up-tempo mode. Adisa's ringbang compositions are faster than any of his earlier experiments—in excess of 130 beats per minute. But the relationship between a song's tempo and its lyrical focus is not a fixed one. That is, there is no rule which insists that an up-tempo song in excess of 130 beats per minute cannot address socio-political concerns. Throughout the development of soca there has been a dispelling of this tendency to associate the "strong" song of commentary with a labored tempo. There are countless songs which have utilized the fast rhythm to accompany socially committed lyrics.

The point is that ringbang carries a distinctive, clear focus in terms of its lyrical text. It emphasizes less "serious" lyrics, and some say it should since the focus of this phenomenon is the drum and rhythm. But this reasoning is potentially loaded with a number of cultural biases in associating the drum with dance and gyration. Since Grant points out that the phenomenon of ringbang has the potential to re-contextualize other texts, it is reasonable to assume that this rhythm can be played on top of "heavier" lyrics as well. At present ringbang has gradually begun to put this possibility into practice (on *Ringbang Rebel Dance*, for example). Grant is insistent that the dance must come first.

I do not intend to engage in any protracted discussion on ringbang's lyrical focus and content, but I consider it important to examine selected ringbang lyrical texts as a way of buttressing the conclusions which I draw here. I will also attempt to comment on the musical text by way of assessing ringbang's potential as a divergent Caribbean music style.

Gabby's "Dr Cassandra" fits into the category of the double entendre composition. This type of composition characterizes a lyrical and stylistic method which has been worked and re-worked by many composers in the calypso art form. In fact, many calypsonians, including Gabby himself, have utilized the metaphor of "doctor(ing)" to re-interpret the goings on between the male and female in intimate situations (i.e., Pompey's "Doctor Doctor"). Gabby's 1960 composition "Heart Transplant" also makes use of this metaphor in exploring the double meaning. "Dr Cassandra" (1994) merely adds to a body of work which has been exploited on numerous occasions in the kai-soca tradition.

I was feelin ill
When I get a house call from Dr Cassandra
Boy she give me pill
Now me whole body feeling better than ever
She give me one injection in my mid section
I didn't have to pay
Then she give me something and tell me swallow
Fever gone right away.

When yuh coming back
Sandra when yuh coming to give me medicine
(Be quiet boy I'm your doctor
I come here to make you better)
When yuh coming back
Sandra when yuh coming to give me medicine
(Be quiet boy I'm your doctor
I come here to make you better)
And then she jook jook jook jook jook jook jook jook
Jook jook jook jook jook jook jook jook
She jook muh here
She jook muh there
She jook muh here
She jook muh there
And then she jook jook jook jook jook jook jook jook
Jook jook jook jook jook jook jook jook

I say doctor please come back quick
Because I can't bear it no longer
Only you could ease how I palpitating
and cool down me pressure
She say how you expect to feel better
When you in such a hurry
I got two mind to stop de treatment
Give yuh ague in your body

She say bye for now boy
I have to fulfil I another appointment
All yuh need is rest and in no time
at all yuh conquer de ailment
(She say take de medicine twice a day
that is de dose I should get
I follow instructions to my surprise
my body fit like a jet)[26]

Were the merits of a kaiso composition judged solely by its selection of theme, freshness of its topic, or exclusivity of lyrics, then Gabby's "Dr Cassandra" might be found greatly wanting. But this concern with the issue of critical appraisal redirects a number of questions in relation to the value judgments which my type of analysis carries and imposes on the ringbang text. Questions such as, "What should privilege one composition which treats a new topic over another composition which deals with a theme that has been done and re-done?" and, "Since ringbang emphasizes the rhythmic component of the work, then is the kind of analysis of lyrical content which I am practicing misdirected and inappropriate?" One may also wonder how to begin to judge compositions like Viking Thundah's "Ring A Ringbang"—its popularity, effectiveness, potency and worth. Can the lyrical text alone form the basis of such an appraisal?

Danca lingua hear/here/hair style
All de girl dem up front
hands in de air and jump
Ohhhhhhhhh

A ring a ring a ringbang
A ring a ring a ringbang
Viking got a new slang
Viking got a new slang

Come catch 'e dust jump up
Come catch 'e dust wine up
Come catch 'e dust hands up
Ringbang style to keep dem jumping up

Watch how Patsy jumping
Rude girl misbehaving
De say fe play de Viking
They love de ringbang rhythm
Feel dem dance hall shaking
Niceness keep on playing
All dem misbehaving

Everybody jamming
Ringbang a de in thing
Jamming in de morning
Niceness a de evening
Everybody jumping
Straight back to da morning
See how dem people jamming
Watch dem bumper shaking
Dem look so inviting
Getting a de feeling
Have de ringbang jamming
Hear de thunder talking

Watch how Angie jumping
Watch how Suzie wining
Rude girl a de new swing
Watch dem bumper bouncing
Look boy wan go test dem
What them think dem doing
All dem a go waist swing
Respect to me girlfriend[27]

Viking Thundah's lyrical texts liberate his songs in a number of ways. These compositions are celebratory in treatment and tone, and they anticipate audience participation during the live performance (partly through the employment of much repetition). "Ring A Ringbang" is a blatant transgression from the serious commentary attributed to kaiso. The lyrics are primarily concerned with celebrating the achievement of a "new slang": ringbang. There is no sense of any concern with lyrical development on a theme. Imagery, metaphor, satire and symbolism—all inexpendable devices for the kaisonian—are not central within this lyrical text. Furthermore, in as far as some soca lyrical texts have tended to treat an incident "in the party" or between some female and male as imposing a framework for developing a narrative dialogue, this particular text does not operate in that mode. It begins to assert its difference even from soca texts. I suggest that Viking's song operates more like some dancehall compositions; those which center the power of the song's persona and the chanter behind the microphone.

Allow me to restate that the kind of approach which my previous analysis deliberately assumes in seeking to isolate the lyrical text from its other performative constituents is formal. That method is inadequate in some ways and distorts the total text of ringbang's overall representation. There is a danger in attempting to separate the lyrical make-up from its musical arrangements. There is even further danger in analyzing ringbang outside the context of the performance event wherein the "text in total" is constituted, that is, when the process of artist-audience interplay is being negotiated. When listening to the compositions which make up *Fire in the Wave* (CD)one realizes that their strength resides in the way the lyrical texts were constructed—to suit their projected performance contexts as well as a certain type of performance moment. The lyrical texts to which I refer can be considered functional and complementary to the overall representation of ringbang. The compatibility of lyrics, performance potentiality, and context comprise the "text in total."

By "text in total" I mean the sum total of components and referents on which a work depends for constituting its disseminative signification. This can refer to a song's lyrics, musical composition, media of realization, intended audience, and market orientations. For example, in relation to *Fire in the Wave* (CD) you can talk of its textness as being made up by the lyrics, musical arrangements (some of which we will examine), market-oriented packaging, and "party" context. The technological devices and instruments employed in the composition, recording, and production of this work comprise an important dimension of its text. For example, the use of modern technological approaches to recording (multi-track) means that we hear sound productions in which a vocalist is simultaneously the lead as well as background vocalist within the same song. This realization foregrounds the text's recorded performance context as displaced. There is an unlimited number of different recording contexts. We know that it is not humanly possible for an individual to sing two distinctly different words or sounds at the same time. Although we hear Gabby providing backup for songs in which he sings lead, we mediate the voices simultaneously by employing a multi-track reading of our own. In experiencing or appreciating the song we have had to negotiate its constructedness by deconstructing the dialogic codes within the final recorded text. The employment of certain technological devices can have hidden or stated codes which affect the way in which a work is constituted in the disseminative stage. Therefore, the lyrical text must be considered in relation to the other constituent, contextual factors which comprise the ringbang's (or any other form of recorded music's) "text in total."

The musical component is of extreme importance to the make-up of ringbang. Grant has made this point earlier in the chapter and the ringbang texts which have been produced so far give substance to his directive. This said, we could conclude this section on the musical features of ringbang since we are in agreement with Grant's statements that the ringbang text foregrounds its rhythmic component. However, there are still some queries which beg to be addressed, namely, ringbang's legitimacy. As a rhythm, how is it going to be different from its co-texts? Is it merely appropriating indigenous rhythms and renaming them? What are the politics surrounding the creation and dissemination of this style?

Grant has acknowledged the intertextual relationship which ringbang shares with other rhythms and phenomena in the Caribbean. For example, in the interview cited above he makes reference to the influences which one could expect a Trinidad ringbang to exhibit. He talks of Trinidad as the mecca of kaiso and makes the point that "they bring the horns." Therefore, a Trinidad ringbang might reveal the appropriation of this horns motif within its composition.

This particular point is buttressed in the 1994 Super Blue track entitled "Jab Molassie." This song is somewhat of a ringbang standard: the drums stand out in the mix and it employs a gaitless snare which is tight (one which slaps you when it is played on to the repeated phrases of "Jab Molassie"). There are other drums which share an equal recorded balance in the rhythm's mix. These other drums (two or three of them) are more resonant. They are tuned much lower than the snare. One might be inclined to say that two of these drums represent the lowest tuned toms of a standard five-piece kaiso drum set. But in terms of the application and treatment of these drum samples on the recorded text, it is evident that they represent the presence of some other percussive set. These drums acquire a status in the mix which is not accorded the drums within the kaiso and soca genres. These two samples are punctuated by the foot drum's depth, creating a pseudo-techno impact. Within this composition the music is stripped of soca's embellishments (i.e., horns, percussive ideophones, membranophones, rhythm guitar, persistent riding bass, and backup vocals), giving birth to a hardcore style. The drums and voice dominate from beginning to end. As the song progresses congas, horns and vocal over-dubs are introduced and play an embellishing role within the song.

Viking Thundah's "Ring A Ringbang" is similar to the above song in that it highlights the drums and is stripped of the musical instruments and components which sustain the rhythmic drive of most soca texts. Its soloist and drums dominate the mix of this composition.

Like "Jab Molassie," "Ring A Ringbang" is built on the repetition of simple, catchy, choric phrases. Like Super Blue, Viking Thundah interprets his lyrics in the singing-cum-chanting mode and with a spirited, aggressive temperament. They attack the microphone. This method has the effect of ascribing a macho potency to the ringbang text. This perception is buttressed by the fact that thus far ringbang's main exponents have been men. Their lyrics have tended indirectly to center the female as object of their "party" exploits. Gabby's "Dr Cassandra" is built on the female's ability to inject the right medicine. In

"Deborah," the female is created primarily for the purpose of giving "de sugar":

> *Oh dear Deborah give me de sugar*
> *I don't care if you give me cancer*
> *I don't care if I die or suffer*
> *Oh dear Deborah give me de sugar*
> *I don't care if you give me disease*
> *I ain't frightened for diabetes*[28]

Although I have been pointing to the similarities between some ringbang texts I want to emphasize that in terms of rhythm it also reveals a number of contrasting styles. For example, not all of these musical texts are as insistent on the drum as Viking Thundah's song. Gabby's "Deborah," for example, places less emphasis on the drum throughout than in most other ringbang songs. Rather, it introduces a bridge-functioning drum encoded segment which I think marks this work as ringbang.

Square One's "Ruk a Tuk Party," unlike most other ringbang texts, is a rich composition with full musical accompaniment and a "live" feel. This song appears less contrived and cosmetic after the final mix down. It carries the weight of a live performance. Though its drums are a central motif, this song is less ostentatious and more convincing in its application of ringbang. It is intertextual in its fusing of ruk-a-tuk, ringbang and soca. This song represents Grant's suggestion that ringbang has a number of regional, international and cultural applications.

Some observations which are being made in the public domain have to do with a belief that ringbang is no different than soca. This debate is potentially inconclusive since the measuring of textual difference in the popular domain is highly subjective and inherently problematic. Perhaps this debate can only really be resolved by time, but by 1998 the movement away from soca, strictly defined, is even more radical.

In making statements of comparison and contrast, I suggest that as a musical text ringbang does draw from kaiso and related genres. They are based on similar musical aesthetics. Ringbang does not profess to be an anti-text of kai-soca. They are more so co-texts, hence their perceived similarities. Ringbang's differ-ence is marked by the absence therein of a number of instruments and instrumentation which comprise the kai-soca idiom. In the realization of their absence, the drum becomes foregrounded to the status of full presence in defining the composition of ringbang. Whereas I have marked the point which both fixes and divides ringbang and soca, there is much more difficulty in bracketing off ringbang and tuk and in deconstructing textual difference within their commodified form and representation.

There is a school of thought that believes Grant is appropri-ating tuk in the name of ringbang. When you listen to Adisa's two ringbang songs released in 1994, they are indeed heavily influ-enced by tuk. They make blatant use of tuk inflections. They contain carefully edited tuk samples. Yet Adisa makes numerous references to ringbang within the lyrics of his songs. This suggests that for him these compositions are indeed ringbang.

In discussion of tuk and ringbang, the following questions must be brought forth: Are tuk and ringbang mutually inclusive categories? Are they interchangeable titles for the similar rhythm? Will audiences become attuned to the practice of referring to the tuk band as the ringbang band? Or are there indeed distinctions between tuk and ringbang, based on features external to the rhythms themselves?

It seems to me that ringbang is much more than merely a rhythm. It seeks to be a philosophy; a way of life. It is a strategy of re-contextualizing and disseminating various regional, cul-tural-specific texts within a re-configured mode. Although Adisa's compositions employ tuk inflections for drum tracks, these drums do not comprise his songs' only motifs. His musical texts operate in tandem with chanting. This practice is not endemic to the tuk tradition, at least not in its contemporary manifestation. Tuk makes use of what some anthropologists call "cries" and "hollas." Adisa's songs cannot be labeled as authentic tuk in their disseminated form. In their final re-presentation they are differ-ent from what can be considered real tuk in terms of vocal and musical performative treatment. If the musical drum tracks with which we are concerned existed by themselves as a distinctive entity (if the rhythm section were stripped to the drum tracks alone), then it could be proposed without doubt that these songs are tuk. But there are a number of other attendant motifs and trans-cultural signs which are present within Ice productions.

I admit that Ice makes much use of the rhythms of tuk (and other rhythms as well), there is no denying this. But there is a distinction between the music of the traditional Barbadian band in its authentic performative context and the approximate rhythm when it has been digitally sampled, edited, fused and packaged. The difference is imposed by the process of re-contextualization through modern techniques of re-presentation. The tension between tuk and ringbang hinges on the dialogic interface between the raw cultural and culture-specific text and the process of its transference into an universally acceptable format, specifically, the process of technological transference of a raw text into the commodified form. It is here that the real debate between tuk and ringbang is located.

NOTES

1 Personal interview with Anthony "Gabby" Carter (1992).

2 Egudu, R.N. "The Igbo Experience." *Oral Poetry in Nigeria.* Edited by Uchegbudam Abalogu (Lagos: Nigeria Magazine, 1981) 247-256.

3 Warner, Keith. *Kaiso! The Trinidad Calypso.* (Washington: Three Continents Press, 1982) 111.

4 "Miss Barbados." First performed by Gabby in 1983 during th Crop Over Festival. Released on *One in De Eye* (album).

5 Cou-cou is the national dish of Barbados.

6 See note 4 above.

7 See note 4 above.

8 "Cadavers." From *One in de Eye* (album).

9 Carter, Anthony "Gabby." "Who Gabby Tink He Is?"

10 "Bow Wow Wow!"

11 Ibid.

12 "De List."

13 "Jack." First performed in 1982 during the Crop Over Festival. Released on *One in De Eye* (album).

14 Stab-out is Bajan for malnourished.

15 See note 9 above.

16 Carter, Anthony "Gabby." "Boots." First performed in 1983 during the Crop Over Festival. Realeased on *One in De Eye* (album).

17 Monti, Franco. *African Masks*. (London: Paul Hamlyn, 1969) 15.

18 Eco, Umberto. "Frames of Comic Freedom." *Carnival!* Edited by Thomas Sabeok (Berlin: Mouton Publishers, 1984) 1-9.

19 Carter, Anthony "Gabby." "Send A Answer Fuh We."

20 Carter, Anthony "Gabby." "Jimmy Swaggart."

21 Ibid.

22 Finnegan, Ruth. *Oral Literature in Africa*. (Nairobi: Oxford University Press, 1970) 92.

23 See note 1 above.

24 "The Investigator's Showtime" by Andrea King. Subsequent references to his comments on ringbang are taken from this interview and from my conversations with Eddy Grant.

25 "Jump in the Ringbang Tide." From *Fire in the Wave* (CD).

26 "Dr Cassandra." From *Fire in the Wave* (CD).

27 "Ring A Ringbang." From *Fire in the Wave* (CD).

28 Carter, Anthony "Gabby." "Deborah." From *Fire in the Wave* (CD).

6 POPULAR BANDS, GOSPEL AND DUB CULTURE

This chapter focuses on three areas of Barbadian music culture which deserve independent consideration and analysis. Although this chapter does not seek to make any direct connection between the three areas of concern here, their inter-connectedness becomes evident and obvious in the final analysis. My consideration of these three phenomena takes place within the context of the 1980s and 1990s. In addition to offering important insights on contemporary Barbadian popular bands, gospel, dancehall and dub culture, this chapter is concerned with the state of the national music entertainment scene, culture and industry leading up to the 21st century.

POPULAR BANDS: TECHNOLOGY AND THE INDUSTRY

Upon examination of the types of songs which dominated the majority of the performance sets of the better known popular bands—Ivory, Saturn, Savage, Spice, Second Avenue, Coalition, Square One, Caribbean Rhythms, Chocolate Affair, Sygnacha, Axis, Pyramid, Syndicate, Sylkk, Swing Full Force, Exodus, Hot Gossip, Artwork, Krosfyah and Pure Gold—throughout the 1980s and 1990s, it can be concluded that they showed a fixation with Top-40 material, interspersed with varying amounts of Caribbean rhythms such as reggae, calypso, dancehall and soca. It is fair to say that popular bands have not been overt exponents of indigenous Barbadian rhythms. But this said, it is still my objective to talk of the contribution of such bands to the music entertainment industry. Furthermore, I think it is also important to examine the types of socio-political, cultural and ideological networks which characterized the entertainment industry of the 1980s and 1990s. It is crucial to look at the types of avenues which were created in the industry as well as economic and other market forces which influenced the directions that many bands in the 1980s and 1990s were forced to take.

A significant contribution of popular bands in the 1980s was their access to and application of music technology. In as much as the 1980s can be said to have been the decade of the birth of digital technology in the music industry worldwide, local bands were constantly in touch with many of these developments. The drum machine had a notable impact. It was in the 1980s when Blue Wave Studios began to employ the linn drum and other types of electronic drum interface. This application also became a common "hookup" for many popular bands by the middle of the 1980s. Bands such as Spice became heavy users of musical instrument digital interface (MIDI). Like Spice, other groups showed a preference for sequencing their music (programming beforehand) and combining live playing with the pre-programmed sequences at the performance moment. Although the introduction and application of this technology fostered a much more polished sound throughout the 1980s and up into the 1990s, in some cases there was blatant misuse of this technology. Many of these cases were noticeable in the gospel arena where some of its leading groups were utilizing the drum machine as the band's engine. In some instances there was noticeable conflict between live drummers and their pre-programmed drum kits. Whereas the drum machine was employed by many bands in the secular domain as a metronomic device, in the gospel arena many groups tended to stretch the performative function of the drum machine, even when it shared the stage with the live drummer. In some instances the drum machine played drum breaks instead of the live drummer. This was the extent of reliance on technological modes of sound generation and automated "virtual" performance.

The introduction of this technology also saw a number of significant changes within the set-up of many popular bands. The electronic drum kit replaced acoustic sets throughout the island. In most cases the skins were replaced with electronic pads by

Simmons, Roland and Yamaha. The extent of the popularity of electronic kits became apparent through an experiment at the Crop Over Festival in the mid-1980s: that of employing an electronic kit, live drummer, and linn drum. The misuse of the linn drum within this context became evident when playback recordings of performances from the national stadium were coded with an intrusive metronome which ticked throughout.

The real impact of the drum machine and digital interface can be summed up in the 1980s trend of doing away with the live drummer and utilizing the drum machine in all contexts. I want to suggest that there were a number of reasons for the supplanting of the live drummer. Some of these were technological and others had to do with economics. With the availability of drum machines and sequencers, many groups saw the possibility of enhancing the sound quality of their bands through the synchronization of drum machines and keyboards. Because drum machines could be connected to the sound system through direct line signals there was no need to employ open microphones for micing the drum set. This meant that there was less likelihood of hiss and outside noises, creating a cleaner, more polished sound. This was a stated objective of many local bands throughout the 1980s and 1990s.

Some groups saw the potential economic advantages of replacing the live drummer. Since many of the local popular bands were making their living by playing the hotel and night club circuit, it became economically sensible to limit the number of personnel within bands. The drum machine was one less performer which had to be paid from a band's earnings after a performance. Second Avenue, Axis, and Sylkk, were the pioneering bands of this type of set-up. Since night club and hotel owners were insistent on the playing of Top-40 songs by local bands, this imposition favored the utilization of drum machines and synthesizers, synchronized through MIDI. Such bands also discarded the guitar. The synthesizer was assigned the function previously assigned to the rhythm guitar.

The minimalist application of technology is therefore a feature of Barbadian music in the 1980s and early 1990s. In making this point I am pointing to a uniformity and conformity in the selection, acquisition and utilization of musical technology. It is possible to trace a number of trends which dominated the local music scene. A number of these trends surrounded such instruments as the Dx7 (keyboard), RX5 (drum machine), and SDS9 (electronic drum kit) At one point or another throughout the 1980s, these instruments were common pieces in most local bands. Many live performances and recordings revealed blatant similarities in terms of voices (keyboard sounds) and samples (pre-recorded sound bites) which were being used with little indication of creativity. Such were the pressures created by an imposing technology and the perception of its infallibility by eager musicians.

These restricted applications of technology were a result of socio-ideological factors. Many bands were restricted in their creativity and experimentation with technology due to media-derived perceptions of what was happening in the industry. This process resulted in an obsession with Top-40 songs and sounds. The 1980s saw the introduction of FM radio in Barbados, an institution which played a telling role in the perpetuation of non-indigenous music and rhythms. The formats of these stations were saturated with non-indigenous forms of music, contributing little to the advancement of Barbados' music throughout their 1980s and 1990s programming. Those who disagree with this conclusion will point to the playing of Bajan calypsos on FM radio but the reality is that this practice is seasonal. The focus of my criticism has to do with the orientation and philosophy of FM radio in Barbados. The formats and play lists of FM radio in the island have and continue to deprive national artists of national, regional and, by extension, international exposure. Some FM radio DJs have shown an indifference to the development of a national music culture industry. Many others have demonstrated an ignorance.

This ignorance characterized the outlook of successive government policy makers vis-a-vis the importance of a national music culture industry. There were no major concessions given to musicians throughout this period. There were no major policies which showed governmental commitment to the future development of the entertainment industry. The relaxing of duties within the recording industry at the Crop Over Festival has proven to be an incentive to some artists, but it is evident that the music entertainment industry is in dire need of sustained policy support and not just selected concessions at periodic intervals. By 1998 this is still the tendency.

A notable feature of Barbadian music as reflected in popular bands from the mid-1980s and into the 1990s has been the search for a style. By this I am referring to an ongoing preoccupation of some bands with acquiring a status based on the dominant rhythmic focus of their repertoire. For example, a group like Square One acquired the label of a soca band based on the high energy performances which culminated many of their sets. This concern with identity became increasingly important in Bajan music in this period. My use of the word *identity* here does not refer so much to any preoccupation by groups with perfecting their own lyrical and musical trademark, rather it refers to the attempts by many bands to locate themselves within the musical camps whose parameters had already been drawn up (i.e., Top-40, soca, reggae, dancehall and pop).

The international music industry's flirtation with world beat in the 1980s impacted some Barbadian bands. Spice & Co. assumed this brand of music (which they featured on their late 1980s and early 1990s albums *A Different World* and *Dance Across The Seas*). Sunsplash, a band in transition around this same period, also experimented in this genre in such songs as "Free" and "Play the Game of Life." But they soon became Splashband, a bona fide reggae band. The evolution of this group from Ivory to Splashband—from pop-rock to roots-reggae—is indicative of a number of attempts at circumventing the music industry's shifting emphasis. With the impact of dancehall in the international music industry and the signing of some reggae and dancehall acts, local bands saw the possibility of gaining access to global audiences through this genre. Splashband's debut album *X-amonk A Music* was met with a lot of excitement and their live sets created a wider youthful following for the group. By the mid-1990s, however, there was every indication that the restructuring of this band was a reflection of the hardships involved in attempting to acquire pan-regional and global recognition. Although reggae bands have been making a comeback on the international scene, the case of Splashband shows the sheer difficulties involved in transferring a national act onto the international scene. The international industry has yet to give serious consideration to soca. Bands of the 1980s such as Caribbean Rhythms and Chocolate Affair would have found difficulties in gaining wider access to markets in spite of their commercial-sounding releases "Don't Stop the Music" and "Funtime." Soca bands have tended to compose and record their material for ethnic markets in the metropolis. The inability of Barbadian bands to get onto the international scene has more to do with the structure and imperatives of the international industry than with the talent and musical ability of Barbadian musicians. Local musicians are undoubtedly skilled and possess the ability and genius which the international industry demands. Management marketing and distribution continue to be the major failings within the local industry.

What would have been the present status of local bands in relation to the international industry if these bands had experimented with indigenous rhythms like tuk and spouge with some vigor? The popular bands of the 1980s and 1990s have paid only token reference to indigenous musical motifs. One wonders whether these bands have not lost out on the opportunity for international recognition, especially throughout the 1980s when the record industry's interest in regional styles (world music) was in its heyday. Could experimentation with spouge and tuk have captured global attention? This is a point to which I return at the conclusion to this book.

By the middle of the 1990s there were a few signs that Barbadian music was gaining a wider audience and greater recognition. The appearance of artists like RPB and John King on major labels like Sony and RCA are occurrences to be observed (though these are not the first). The perpetuation of this trend places the island's music industry in good stead. But these occurrences are in no way major achievements when one considers the volume of Barbadian musicians who are demonstrating equal national standing without rising to international recognition. Involvement of local artists with major labels is not a new thing for Bajan musicians. Artists like Jackie Opel and Lou Kirton have appeared on or had close dealings with Island, Columbia and CBS. Charles D. Lewis signed to Polygram in the beginning of the 1990s. His contribution to Barbadian music has gone relatively unnoticed by the entertainment industry at home, though his recent return to his native island could signal the utilization of this talent (and others like his) in creating a base for engaging the international music industry. Presently though, the absence of a collective sensibility and orientation in approaching the international industry and markets does not augur well for Barbados' music industry. Governmental cultural planners do not realize this.

DENOMINATIONAL POLITICS IN
THE NAME OF THE GOSPEL

In referring to Barbadian gospel music it is possible (and perhaps desirable) to segment the number of contributing strains which have given substance to this genre within Barbados. Although I do not intend to deal extensively with the several forms of religious music, I want to at least make mention of some of them here before I do actually go on to focus on what I will call Barbadian popular gospel.

Any in-depth treatment of gospel music in Barbados must make mention of the impact of European music on the forms of music which we can now come to categorize as being Barbadian. European choral and choir forms have had a tremendous influence—one which has filtered down through an exported Anglo-Catholic litany and worship format. Anglican congregations in Barbados have for years worshipped to similar songs as their British counterparts. It is only in the latter half of the 1980s that there was any conscious attempt to "Caribbeanize" the litany and some of the music which accompanies worship. However, the Anglican-inspired form which derives from the European tradition still has a strong presence within Barbados.

Choral and choir music within this mold is also common to some less established denominations, like some Pentecostal assemblies. Up until the late 1960s a form of choral music was quite strong outside the strictly defined contexts of religious worship. The village choir was a popular entity within many communities. These choirs were part of the main attraction at Barbadian service-o-songs. Their songs were predominantly religious and reflected the similar treatment and performance as given to these songs within the strictly religious context of church.

In the 1970s, with the rise in popularity of spouge and the proliferation of combos within the secular domain, there was also a movement towards other forms and media of expression within the religious sphere. It is possible to trace some of the developments of Barbadian music through its mirroring of developments in the music industry abroad, particularly in the United States. Barbadian gospel has borrowed heavily from that of the United States in the 1980s and 1990s. In the same way that American gospel in the 1960s and subsequently derived significant influence from its secular co-tradition, Barbadian popular gospel has likewise reflected a number of significant influences from its own secular co-tradition.

Throughout the 1970s and during the heyday of spouge, Barbadian gospel reflected a relatively vibrant engagement with this indigenous rhythm. People like Joseph Niles of the Consolers were staunch performers of gospel in the spouge idiom. Other performers, like sister Margreta Marshall and Ann Riley, were practitioners of this type of gospel music. The association of Joseph Niles with the Consolers was a significant event in Barbadian gospel. The fifteen-year relationship produced a consistent series of sound recordings. As a solo artist Joseph Niles recorded a string of albums and 45s beginning with "This Train" (1967). The 1990s found this artist showing a preference for Caribbean rhythms in the up-tempo style. Throughout the decades his formula has been one of selecting familiar spirituals, which he has performed to the rhythms of calypso, reggae and spouge. Arguably, it is his 1985 album *Feast of Belshazzar* which represents his closest approximation to a commercial sound. This album benefited particularly from the brilliant contribution by the trumpeter Ricky Brathwaite. But after this release, one noticed a re-commitment to the earlier formula which is characterized by his outstanding voice (in the mix) and a lively raw musical accompaniment.

Gospel music activity in the 1980s and 1990s can be considered to have made a number of important contributions to Barbados' entire musical development. It is problematic to attempt an appraisal of a genre such as gospel. For one thing, how do you assess the contribution of a practice whose aims are considered (in some cases) to be spiritual? What I am trying to highlight here is the difficulty of finding a criteria for accessing gospel music's achievements. Let me say at this point that this section is not concerned with the phenomenon of religious affectation. I am not overly concerned here with counting the number of converts who were made to Christianity throughout the 1980s and 1990s. But perhaps some individuals might say that therein lies the true criteria for assessing gospel's relative successes or failures. It is not my intention to dismiss this argument, for it is a significant one, however, that kind of emphasis could reveal other problems or degenerate into arguments surrounding the measurement of the actual volume of converts and so on. That is a debate which falls outside the objectives of this book.

It is less problematic to talk of gospel in terms of macro-societal practice and impact. For example, we can in hindsight theorize on its greater societal impact as a result of the creation of a gospel music concert culture within the 1980s and early 1990s. And we can even proceed to theorize on the apparent decline of this cultural core by 1992 or 1993. My reference to a gospel music concert culture is deliberate since I think that this phenomenon represents one of the more notable developments surrounding gospel music and points to its direct impact on Barbadian society. Barbadian audiences in the 1980s and 1990s engaged in a number of performance practices which they enacted in the gospel music arena. This cultural phenomenon was at the point of greatest impact around the late 1980s.

Perhaps I need to clarify these statements, some of which might seem non-complimentary of gospel music practice in Barbados throughout the 1980s and 1990s. What I am pointing to as a set of performance practices in the gospel music arena is merely a reference to the creation and expansion of a certain relationship between performers and audiences within the gospel music context. I am also making reference to the perpetuation of a number of given performance practices which characterized Barbadian gospel in this period. The Saturday evening concert context became a central point of contact for gospel artists and their audiences. It is within that particular context that there was developed a set of performance practices which became familiar through repeated enactment. The staging of these gospel concerts saw the development of set procedures of performing, composing and disseminating the gospel.

Many weekend gospel concerts in the 1980s and 1990s featured the same gospel acts, rearranged in order of appearance (though it was possible to predict the order of performers). One common practice had to do with the selection and performance of current catchy choruses by performers and invoking expressive participation. Another common practice, primarily of chorales and choirs, was the tendency towards over-improvisation. Such performance tendencies featured the repetition of phrases, and even individual words, for as many times as performers saw fit. Audiences demanded the execution of these excesses and their performing servants willfully carried them out on a regular basis.

The impact of these types of performances (which became codified features of live gospel) transferred into the recorded context. Recordings of the 1980s and 1990s begin to show signs of this formulaic gospel. It is useful to listen to recordings of past choir festivals; they reflect a determination to transmit the practices of the live performance into the recorded format. The live performance was highly privileged in Barbadian gospel.

Unfortunately, the live performance context was over-privileged at the expense of recordings and the recorded text. This has resulted in a noticeable imbalance between a vibrant art form in the live setting and the relative absence of studio-derived recordings. The number and volume of carefully produced gospel recordings over the past fifteen years is markedly small. The consistent producers of gospel recordings over this period were Joseph Niles, the Silvertones, and, to some extent, the Gospel Comforters and Promise. It is possible to access some of the nationally popular chorales through compilations of choir festival performances. Although a group like the New Testament National Chorale ruled the gospel music scene for a number of years in the 1990s, there is little by way of recordings to reflect the extent of their impact and dominance.

I am not at all suggesting that the tendency to privilege the live performance is the prime reason for the relative absence of studio recordings. The absence of substantial amounts of recordings is partly a result of economics. It also reflects the limited outlook of gospel acts within Barbados. This dominant attitude in the gospel music arena constitutes an indifference to the international music industry and its demands—that sound recordings supplement the growth and expansion of the industry. Most gospel acts were content to place sole emphasis on executing effective performances in the live context in front of hundreds of patrons at weekend concerts. Perhaps it is within this context—more so than in any other area—that the greatest contribution of gospel to Barbados' entertainment scene has been made.

Although I have been insisting on a number of shortcomings within gospel music practice throughout the 1980s and 1990s, the fact remains that gospel music has had a marked impact on the culturescape of Barbados in the recent past. Before I go on to suggest some of the other ways in which this contribution was meaningful, I must point out that some gospel artists have had to exist and practice their art under harsh conditions; in conditions much more severe than those of their secular counterparts. In no other area is this more true than in the area of getting patrons and financing a bands' upkeep. Whereas local secular bands could depend on the hotel circuit as a regular source of income, local gospel bands had to depend on a $50 appearance fee for their once-a-week performance if they were lucky. So although this section of the book tends to point to a number of shortcomings within gospel at a macro-societal level, it is ever conscious of the undying efforts which individual musicians and especially local individual bands and band members were making at the micro-level.

It must be concluded that gospel music has served a functional role within Barbadian society. Gospel has had a pivotal position in addressing and shaping a significant portion of society's socio-philosophical sensibilities. I am not saying that gospel in the 1980s and 1990s was the greatest carrier of social values, but gospel certainly did create a sizable audience, and hence it spoke to a significant portion of the population. Gospel offered itself as an alternative to attractions such as drugs, crime and materialism. A little later on I will make some reference to the lyrical content of gospel's "alternative," as expressed through songs. But first let us discuss the functional role of gospel in Barbadian society.

The gospel domain provided an outlet for self-expression for an increasing number of youths throughout the 1980s and 1990s. Some of these youths were or became musicians or singers. Many more of them became occasional or frequent patrons at gospel events. The gospel music domain became a context for social intercourse between many individuals. By the late 1980s the gospel scene was on the verge of creating rivaling fans of leading groups. Whereas certain commentators saw this as a negative trend, the reality was that this development pointed the way towards raising the standard of presentation.

This period in the development of gospel in Barbados was characterized by the formation of numerous new performing chorales, choirs, bands and individual artists. Of all these categories it was the chorales which were most responsible for attracting larger audiences to gospel throughout the 1980s and 1990s. The expressiveness and improvisations of these groups attracted many onlookers. Many gospel events therefore featured such chorales, whose presentations tended to be celebratory. This performance tendency was appealing to a growing audience. It is on these types of performances that the strength and effectiveness of gospel acts came to be measured by audiences and media critics alike. The type of effectiveness to which I am referring relates to visible impact on audiences created primarily through the vocal rendition of gospel performers. Audiences were captivated by the chorales' spirited vocal gymnastics. This had to do with a style of vocalization where chorales built up excitement through the repetition of lyrical motifs (words which they worked and re-worked) very often at the ending of songs. That is the point at which they moved into a series of post-song improvisations. It is these improvisations which effectively became the focal point of performances.

I should make mention here of the band the Redemptions, which had really been creating this kind of stir in audiences prior to the proliferation of dynamic chorales. It is on account of the spontaneous and vibrant renditions of many groups throughout the 1980s and 1990s that audiences were inclined to connect with gospel. The degree of this influence cannot be understated, neither should the mode of its realization be ignored in performance studies which focus on the Caribbean region.

A major deficiency of gospel music in Barbados throughout the 1980s and 1990s is the absence of innovation and originality. Whereas chorales were turning concert venues out, they were reliant on performing covers of North American songs. There was no progressive movement within gospel towards self-definition with a view towards wider regional and perhaps international identification. Creativity and originality, far from being promoted, were discouraged at a number of different levels. One notices a recent tendency of paying homage to Caribbean rhythms by some gospel performers. There is, however, an absence of socially committed and culturally relevant lyrics within most of these performances. Caribbean gospel has not explored the association between religio-spiritual and other types of liberation. The absence of this dimension in regional gospel continues to be a major failing. The lyrical focus of gospel performers is still centered on overworked metaphors and hackneyed phrases. The ongoing practice of distancing local gospel from socio-cultural reality perpetuates amicable relations between gospel's controllers and a conservative political order.

The preferences of live audiences influenced and dictated the playlists of radio stations. With relatively few recordings to choose from, the playing of local gospel was sparse. There were some genuine attempts at giving exposure to gospel's diversity. In this regard, the efforts of Emmanuel Joseph stand out. His persistence in highlighting local gospel and his concern for the overall development of local gospel (as demonstrated during his stint on the radio show Vibrations), is unequaled in recent Barbadian radio. The efforts by Faith FM, CBC and VOB do not begin to reflect such genuine concern for all facets of local gospel.

The absence of originality and creativity in gospel over this contemporary period is a major failing of Bajan gospel. Gospel's perpetuation of sameness in terms of musical and lyrical texts is a reflection of the pressures which were exerted on gospel's practitioners by forces both within and outside of the gospel arena. There was a noticeable tendency of some audiences to resist attempts at original composition. The root of this attitude stems from an ideological confrontation which was being played out in Barbadian society. In order to better understand the power dynamics which were and continue to be in operation and connected with gospel, it is important to examine the relationship between gospel's practitioners and what I call denominational agencies. The nature of this relationship is one of denominational power bases in control of gospel's exponents.

A careful examination of the association between gospel performers and denominational centers reveals a submissive dependency on organizations by gospel practitioners. Since gospel acts continue to be dependent on a denominational base for patronage and their sustenance, the music of these groups is wont to reflect the preferences and directives of their denominational bases. When it is further revealed that certain denominations are known to hold council with other interests within secular society then we begin to understand the implications of this in the shaping of gospel in contemporary Barbadian society.

Since groups and performers are not independent, gospel has had to carry on a practice in confinement. It is a known fact that certain denominations do prohibit some gospel bands from playing within their assemblies. This is considered a case of denominations exercising their aesthetic preference and selection. But the deeper reality is that this discriminatory practice is a political act. It reflects the power of control which denominational boards have wielded over gospel throughout the 1980s and 1990s. Apart from excluding some gospel performances there has been a tendency in other denominations to suppress performances which demonstrate radically different or creative input. The 1980s and 1990s have also brought to the surface pressures associated with assuming relative autonomy within the gospel arena. Groups, such as the north-based Persuaders, experienced the difficulties of not possessing a denominational base. Such groups, though talented, were marginal if only on account of lacking a fixed denominational center.

There were also other attempts at assuming varying levels of autonomy. Some groups, bands in particular, were exploring a series of relationships with their denominational bases. While they worshipped in these assemblies on main worship days, they were exploring separate programs outside of worship time. Promise is an interesting case of study in this regard. In the early 1990s, although its members were associated with denominational bases, Promise embarked on an intensive program of outreach music. This orientation gave birth to *This is the Day* (cassette). There is a direct correlation between their outward-looking autonomous philosophy and the waning of their popularity, especially within the gospel mainstream. Also significant is the stylistic shift of their music around this time (its approximation to what I call subversive gospel) to a form which goes beyond the cliché of the formulaic tendencies which I referred to earlier.

Although Promise was at the forefront of mainstream gospel within this era in terms of their visibility, it was really other groups who were more subversive and engaged in the "gospel of confrontation." I am referring to a number of performance and musical digressions from mainstream gospel practice. A group like Reaction (prior to its declension around 1994) was engaged in a number of technological performance innovations through which they used digital interface without apologies. The short-lived group Visions challenged the status quo in a different way at the end of the 1980s. With Mark Sandiford as keyboardist and vocalist they presented an aggressive style of gospel with rock-styled guitar, and socially conscious and challenging lyrics. Their level of intensity is equaled and surpassed only by early New Connections, and Wisdom to a lesser extent. The perpetuation of Vision's music in Barbadian gospel would have posed a challenge not only to secular society, but to the gospel arena, its coterie, and their closely guarded performance formulae.

Project Band (Project H&T) was another group which posed a number of challenges to the institutional stagnation of Barbadian gospel music. This group insisted on performing almost total original music. Their 1991 cassette reflected their commitment to originality. Like other groups in the latter half of the 1980s, they moved away from the mainstream practice of "weekend gospel" and embarked on a series of performances at strategic locations in communities. Unlike most of these groups which still maintain binding links to the mainstream, Project Band has persisted in a commitment to autonomous practice outside of the restrictive controls which characterize gospel's denominational hegemony in Barbados.

The mid-1990s has brought little indication that the stranglehold on gospel is being loosened. There is even greater control by dominant elements. The recent thrust into gospel tourism reveals the extent of this greater control. The recurrence of a core group of performers at government sanctioned "festivals" shows the degree to which the gospel's total dissemination is being hampered in contemporary Barbados.

DANCEHALL AND DUB

Dancehall and dub in the 1980s threw up a number of interesting developments. Names like Kid Site, Fat Man, I-Farrell, Mike Richards, Peter Ram, and L'il Rick were the major exponents of chanting to the rhythms of the Caribbean. Within the dancehall forum one can point to Jesse James' "Dub is the Force" as signaling the introduction and rise of dancehall in Barbados. Shane Boodhoo's (Sounds Gud) production was a forerunner to the subsequent attempts at employing the dancehall aesthetic within the Bajan context. Although dancehall and dub are not indigenous art forms to Barbados (and so should have no significant place in a book like this), the fact remains that this book has from its beginning stressed its imperative of examining those forms of music which are practiced in Barbados.

In the 1980s, dancehall became the preferred music of Barbadian youth culture. The impact of Jamaican artists like Yellow Man, Tiger, Lovindeer, Shabba Ranks, and Buju Banton resounded throughout the decades of the 1980s and 1990s. The music of Jamaican culture infiltrated the airwaves, dances, fairs, festivals and live shows—at times featuring the artists themselves.

The Barbadian response to the infectious rhythms and chanting of its fellow island practitioners saw the emergence of its own local chanters. It is significant that Jesse James' "Dub is the Force" was commenting on the phenomenal impact which the art form was making on Barbadian culture. Jesse James' song was well-received, though it never achieved the measure of respect accorded to recordings coming out of Jamaica. Here I am referring to the attitude of DJs, radio jocks, and live audiences to this Bajan adaptation. In retrospect it can be concluded that Barbadian dancehall on the whole suffered a similar reception. It was often seen as subordinate to the "real" tradition which was being practiced in Jamaica and, later on, in the United States and the United Kingdom.

I do not want to suggest that local Barbadian dancehall artists were not making an impact on the music entertainment and culture scene of Barbados—far from it. As live performers, DJs like Fat Man created a tremendous impact at many sessions. Fat Man in particular was featured on an early 1980s record with the calypsonian, Pompey. He chanted on *Rockers Festival* (record). This was one of the first authentic attempts at incorporating the dancehall chanting mode into the performance context of calypso in Barbados, and perhaps anywhere else in the Caribbean. The National Cultural Foundation sponsored the Farley Hill concert as part of Barbados' Crop Over Festival. The foundation was also instrumental in exposing the talents of some dancehall DJs. The competition at Farley Hill catapulted the renown of DJs like Kid Site. Apart from performing in the live context, Kid Site went on to record a series of dancehall songs which received favorable response from varying quarters. Arguably, his mid-1980s "Can't Find Hall" was his most popular song in the dancehall and dub idiom.

The most significant development within Barbadian dancehall took place around the latter part of the 1980s and stretched into the 1990s. When L'il Rick released his song "De Youts," the response to it was unprecedented in the history of Barbadian dancehall. It also became popular in the neighboring islands. A number of things were significant about this song: First, it featured "conscious" lyrics. It addressed the declining standards of Caribbean youths and Caribbean youth culture. The song's central line was the refrain of "me nah know how de youths get so," which expressed the reaction of the general public to many disturbing youth trends such as drug abuse. Another significant feature of the L'il Rick composition was its employment of the Barbadian nation language and its intonation. Whereas earlier Barbadian chanters had been using Barbadian words and references within their songs, L'il Rick, and then Peter Ram took the Bajan components to a new level. The early 1990s was then to witness an experimentation in what could be called Bajan dub.

Before I go on, let me make a point of clarification with respect to the terms *dub* and *dancehall*, and my use of these terms in this book. The purists and academics would situate dub as the older variant of chanting performed by the likes of I Roy. Dub usually includes "conscious" lyrics. Dancehall is commonly regarded as the much later practice which is more commercially oriented and associated with practitioners such as Yellow Man and Shabba Ranks. In common everyday usage, particularly in Barbados and in the eastern Caribbean, there is little distinction between dancehall and dub as musical stylistic labels. In this book I am myself using the terms quite interchangeably.

Chanters like L'il Rick and Peter Ram were at the forefront of this new brand of Bajan dub which was characterized by the overt use of the Bajan dialect and accompanying "conscious" lyrics. (I am referring to the music recordings of these artists since there were differences between the recorded texts and some live performances, particularly in relation to lyrical content.) Live performances and other non-public oriented lyrics tended towards slackness on occasions. But in their recorded tracks, L'il Rick and Peter Ram produced a consistent series of Bajan dub tracks which were responsible for stemming the tide of negative responses towards this reggae sub-genre.

Songs such as "Turn it Down," "We Country," "Police and Rasta," and "We ABC" by L'il Rick, and "Dangerous Disease (AIDS)" and "Quick Sand" by Peter Ram featured lyrics of social consciousness performed with a noticeably Bajan cadence. This particular movement within Bajan dub won the art form some respect in a number of conservative circles. This brand of music certainly brought Bajan dub to mainstream Barbados. It crept on to the play lists of AM radio on both CBC and VOB. So popular was a song like L'il Rick's "De Youths" that some clerics were basing the subject of their sermons on the song's particular lamentation, and politicians were quoting from it as well.

There were other significant contributions to this style of Barbadian dub. Some are found on *Lethal Hits*, a compilation which features some of Barbados' best chanters. Other songs like Gunny Ranks and Ninja Man's "Man Rehab," Daddy Plume's "Big up Escape," and Adowa's "Acid Rain" were insistent on addressing social ills.

This style of Barbadian dub, however, only "ruled" for approximately three years. In 1994 there were signs that Barbadian dancehall artists were abandoning this style. There was a conscious reversion to dancehall's "international style" and Jamaican cadence, and an absence of significant lyrical consciousness. The reasons for this are varied. As some of the practitioners of this early 1990s Bajan dub have revealed: conscious lyrics don't sell. Whereas mainstream Barbados showed tolerant appreciation of the early 1990s experiments, the sales of these recordings were not healthy enough to encourage the perpetuation of this style.

The annual competition and show called Revo-dub-olution continued to build on the conscious focus in Barbadian dub. Successive competitions have thrown up a number of creative performers and socially committed lyrical texts. To some extent it has exposed a number of local chanters who are still committed to maintaining a Bajan cadence. Papa Dutch and Lilee Ranking are but two chanters who show signs of this style. For the most part the Jamaican, or international, style rules, though in some cases there is much switching between local, regional and international cadences. This is an interesting phenomenon which begs for further research.

Coterminous with the developments which I have been referring to all along, there has been a counter-movement. I have tended to pay closer attention to the recorded tracks (those which have been made accessible to the wider society) but the alternative rude boy style still rules, especially within the live and the underground contexts. The underground distribution and dissemination of slackness has persisted within the minibus culture and continues to flourish in the present ZR culture. Minibuses and ZR vehicles are names given to privately owned transport vehicles in Barbados. They are capable of carrying between sixteen and forty passengers. There has been a tendency by the young people to frequent these vehicles which have encouraged the playing of loud suggestive music and have prompted other kinds of deviant activites associated with youth culture. It is within this underground practice that the female voice surfaces within Barbadian dancehall. The thematic focus of many of these transgressive dancehall performances is on sexual encounters. There are many confrontational scenarios between the male and female in these songs. These might be said to reflect the larger confrontation which is taking place between the sexes in other domains of Barbadian society.

Closely related to the art form and the culture of dancehall and dub is rhythm poetry. In Barbados throughout the 1980s and 1990s there have been a number of notable developments within this genre as well. These developments have had some impact on the music entertainment scene of the nation. Rhythm poets such as Winston "I" Farrell and Adisa Andwele have been at the forefront of musical experiments within the genre of perfor-mance poetry.

Rhythm-based artists such as Ricky "Babu" Parris and Rashiv Foster have kept this particular art form alive in Barbados for some time. It is with the dreadlocked I-Farrell, though, that the wider national awareness to the musical possibilities of this art form were realized. This came about largely because of his venturing into studio recordings. Farrell's "De Bus Man" achieved a considerable degree of popularity throughout Barbados. Of particular note was Farrell's incorporation of the tuk rhythm within the recorded version of this song. His song predates Poonka's experiment with calypso and tuk rhythms by a few years and it also pointed the way for later experiments by Adisa.

Other musical experiments by Farrell were tried with calypso, soca and reggae in such songs as "Minibus Hustle," "Twenty one and Moving On," and "Black Woman." But it was his earlier song which demonstrated the potential mass appeal that chanted poetry composed to the rhythms of Barbados could generate. Farrell did not go on to develop this initial experiment with any consistency though he remained quite visible as a performer up into the 1990s. *African Lion on the Loose* (1992 cassette) has been his most ambitious contribution to this art form and to Barbadian music within the 1990s. Although the lyrical content on this release is politically and socially engaging (he addresses a number of national problems and situations) it does not reveal any concerted effort at re-igniting his initial interest in tuk or any other indigenous Bajan rhythmic form. There are a number of exciting musical interpretations of reggae on the release, as well as some successful attempts at rhythmic fusion.

An important point which should be made by way of comparing the rhythm poetry art form with its sister practice of dub in Barbados is the fact that Bajan rhythm poets have tended to hold truer to the Barbadian nation language.

Adisa Andwele has made a significant contribution to rhythm poetry throughout the late 1980s and in the 1990s. He brought a greater sense of professionalism to the art form. He appeared with his own band, Re-emergence, and assumed a pop-styled presentation on stage, that is, with choreographed movements and tightly rehearsed musical and vocal renditions. His signing to Clappers Records and his exploration of the music video form are other important developments in the 1990s. His other most notable contribution has been his experiments with Caribbean rhythms and, in particular, with Bajan rhythms. For example, he performed the song "Uh Come Back Now" during 1992 to the infectious rhythms of spouge. He has signed to Ice and continues to demonstrate a commitment to indigenous forms. One can only look on in anticipation of the new level to which Ice Records will take this and similar artists who continue to perform in the singing-cum-chanting mode.

7 CONCLUSION

I want to conclude this book by making a number of observations and comments in relation to the two indigenous rhythms of Barbados and their place within the soundscape of Barbados' future. Whereas tuk has acquired a lifeline through its fusion with soca and ringbang, spouge's influence has not carried through and appears to have less hope of being perpetuated.

Tuk's rhythmic, metrical and temporal characteristics have been misinterpreted, misrepresented and under-represented in many cases within contemporary applications. Post-1980 experimentation with tuk by musicians, popular bands, and those who operate within the digital domain have limited and restricted the wider possibilities of tuk as a musical style. The majority of songs which have incorporated tuk have fallen within the broadly defined genre of calypso.

Square One's "Special" is the best example of a recorded track which has attempted to do something new with tuk's rhythmic style. It is a slow love groove which does not overstate the influence of tuk. Its tuk-like drums are not centered in terms of their gain or volume level in the mix, but the drum's influence is stated through the reproduction of carefully chosen, edited and recorded drum "voices."

For the most part, composers and arrangers have not conceived of the wider application of tuk beyond soca and other extant Caribbean music forms. Contemporary applications of tuk do not reflect the tuk band's capability of playing other cultural rhythms.

Barbadian musicians who have an eye on the international industry and its market should take the opportunity to explore and exploit the fusion of tuk and mainstream music styles in pop and rock. Songs like Tears For Fears' "Shout" are an example of the wider possibilities for tuk.

Finally, in relation to tuk, more emphasis should be placed on the tonal and textural manifestation of the tuk band. Instead of greater emphasis on rhythmic and metrical properties, composers, arrangers, engineers and producers should begin to analyze and explore the unique sound which the tuk band and its various instruments reproduce, especially since in this digital age there is much scope for sampling the tuk band and its instruments. By doing this musicians can have edited samples of individual or collective tuk instruments at their disposal as sound bites which they can readily incorporate, manipulate and reshape within as many digital set-ups and contexts as desired. As I was intimating about Square One's "Special," music forms such as tuk need not be identified solely by rhythmic focus if it has other tonal characteristics to provide definition. Although I have been referring to its drums as being tuk-like, Eddy Grant defines the song as ringbang säf.

The future of spouge, based on what is taking place in contemporary practice and performances, appears less promising than that of tuk. In the early 1990s there was a renewed interest in spouge. There have been a number of attempts in recent history to re-engage with spouge, but these attempts were limited in success in terms of stimulating an ongoing practice. Richard Stoute's 1985 "Mr. Rich Man" sold fewer than one hundred copies. Recordings like *Spouge Revival* (album), re-issued 1970s music by Wirl, and fusions with soca by people like Tony "Commander" Grazette have not realized any significant reinterpretation or revival of spouge.

Spouge has remained submerged in some of the music which comes out of Barbados. In a future study I will explore this aspect in much more depth. For the present let me summarize by saying that there are noticeable manifestations of spouge and spouge-related motifs in the music played and recorded by Barbadian artists. How much of this influence is consciously created, and how much of it is created unknowingly is a question for my next work.

In the earlier sections of this book I introduced the notion that Barbados has for most its history been regarded as the Caribbean island with the least to offer by way of a vibrant indigenous culture. This perception has been changing rapidly because of many of the phenomena which I have touched on. Currently in the calypso arena, Barbados is regarded as a major innovative force. The projection of a new dance-oriented style like ringbang is largely responsible for this. Raggasoca, or a fusion of reggae and soca, is the other sub-genre which is making a great impact. Red Plastic Bag's massive hit "Ragga Ragga" best exemplifies the style and scope of this form. The song became a huge success and was taken up by Sony for a compilation, *Dancepool*, which also features singles by the likes of Selena. It has been recorded in more than six different languages. Barbados is regarded as the hub of propulsion of these new trends. However, one senses that the nation is unprepared for this occurrence. I say this because there is little indication that there will be a concerted effort to engage these new styles in a systematic and conscience way with a view to projecting and developing them. This is the same kind of vacillation which plagued the industry after the rise of spouge. Barbadian associations which have an interface with music have not seen it fit to put these new developments on their agendas. The major players within the entertainment scene have preferred to adopt a "let the music play" policy. In a way, they are suggesting that artistic creativity and musical development should not be legislated. And they are right. But at the same time there must also be a consolidation of artists.

The history of Barbadian music and culture reveals that in every period of development there has been a laissez-faire approach. This approach has been derived from a colonial system which sought to negate the creative sensibility of African-Barbadians. The vestiges of that mentality still impact the culture today. In the absence of a sober methodical engagement with its own culture the nation continues to suffer greatly, so that many of the developments which have been referred to are built on a fragile foundation. There is still no attempt to conduct programs of education which put the culture of Barbados in perspective. Many artists are therefore under-prepared ideologically and "politically." When I say politically, I refer to the need for local artists to be aware of the set-up of music and culture discourse in the Caribbean and beyond. It is evident that the perception of Barbadian culture as being traditionally borrowed has fed through Caribbean discourses and into the international domain. Barbadian artists cannot operate within a regional or global market effectively unless they come to terms with politics. They must come to terms with the process of this critique as well. It should become evident that any true acceptance of Barbadian musical production must be fought for not only at the level of the performer and the performance, but even more importantly, at the level of critical discourse.

Barbados has been written out of much of the critical discussion on Caribbean culture. Caribbean criticism has acknowledged the creativity of such literary contributors as the Marxist intellectual George Lamming, and Kamau Brathwaite, and has given limited consideration to Austin Clarke, Bruce St. John and Timothy Callender. Other writers like Jeanette Layne Clark and Tony Kellman are even more obscure. Dramatists like Earle Warner and performers like Tony Thompson are on the fringes of academic discourses within their respective genres and spheres of engagement. I have mentioned these individuals by way of suggesting that the tendency to give only reverential mention to Barbadian musicians is symptomatic of an overall tendency within Caribbean cultural discourse. In 1996 at the Conference on Caribbean Culture, I suggested that the origins of a bona fide fusion of reggae and calypso predate Byron Lee and the Dragoneers' 1985 experiments in a song like "Girly Girly." There was resistance to the suggestion that such a style had been recorded in Barbados in 1983 in Pompey's "Rockers Festival" featuring the dub chanter Fat Man. It is not surprising that a number of academic publications which give voice to artists composing in the genres of calypso and reggae are confined to Jamaica and Trinidad. This has nothing to do with the fact that some of these publications are either published in or have as their editors individuals from the said territories. But it is inconceivable that current anthologies and critiques can ignore the contribution and skill of artists like Beckett in St. Vincent, King Short

Shirt of Antigua, Pep and Herb Black and Pelee and Invader and Boo Hinkson of St. Lucia, Ajamu of Grenada, and a long list of Barbadian composers. As the art forms within other areas of the region thrive it will be impossible to ignore this widening of the discursive domain.

But let me not discount the contribution of those bands and artists who in most recent times are fighting in the trenches, so to speak. Presently, select groups and individual artists have earned some measure of respect for themselves and for Barbados. Krosfyah (then spelled Crossfire) began to blaze a trail of popularity from around 1994. They have risen to prominence through competent management and marketing and fresh arrangements. Phil Phillips and Nicolas Brancker have been pivotal figures. The group began by playing for "free" on the road during Trinidad's carnival. This gained them recognition for the single "Climax" as well as for their musical abilities. The projection of lead vocalist Edwin Yearwood as a solo act has also significantly enhanced the popularity of Krosfyah. He was second in the Caribbean song contest, and in 1995 won the Calypso Monarch title, the First Party Monarch title in Barbados, and the Tune of the Crop prize. There was a significant younger following of calypso and Crop Over on account of his involvement. This paralleled the invasion of new patrons in 1982 when Red Plastic Bag first entered the national calypso arena. The popularity of Krosfyah's CD, *Ultimate Party Pump Me Up*, in 1997 selling in excess of 50,000 copies and going gold in Canada is a significant event.

Square One is undoubtedly the most energetic and "tightest" sounding live band of the 1980s and 1990s. They are a close-knit band which has kept all its original members for over ten years of its existence. In the early 1990s the band formed a closer association with Ice Records for whom they produced a limited number of songs, and with some success. But it was in 1996 when they left the Ice label to embark on a more prolific and spontaneous career in terms of recordings that they found greater acceptance and popularity locally and regionally. Their association with Ice Records had been bringing them recognition and respect in other global domains throughout Europe, but they were fighting regionally (for a long time) to become not just a well-loved band but a "monster band." In truth, it is fair to say that their new-found impetus and fame can be traced back to 1995 when still with Ice which produced the song "Ringbang Pickeney." This song introduced the female vocalist as she made a half-menacing invitation to "get on stage!" Subsequent vocal duties on this track were, however, assigned to Anderson "Young Blood" Armstrong, whose rendition augments the vocal aggression which signifies ringbang. In a way, the band's subsequent productions away from Ice Records seems to be a re-visitation and revision of that track. There began to be a fuller projection of Allison Hinds thereafter. She then took over center stage as a calypso/soca/ringbang vocalist. In 1996, with Allison Hinds on lead vocals, the band copped the title of Tune of the Crop winner and its female vocalist was a close second in the Party Monarch finals. In 1997 she turned the tables on Krosfyah's Edwin Yearwood at the Party Monarch competition and shared Tune of the Crop honors with him with her Rameses Browne penned "In the Meantime." Their 1996 and 1997 CDs, *Four Sides* and *Sweetness* (which together contain over thirty songs) have been very popular in the tradi-tional markets as well as in other markets like Suriname and the French-speaking Caribbean. In fact, in late 1997 the songs "Raggamuffin," "Aye Yae Yae," "In the Meantime" and "Con-troller" were competing for poll position on selected charts throughout the region.

Coalishun (formerly Coalition) also took on an enhanced status as a marketable party band. Their tampering with the spelling of their names reflected their new status and focus as The New Coalishun. Their 1996 CD, *Kicking Up Dust*, and their 1997 CD, *Maximum Skin Out*, marked an increase in their popularity. The presence of three strong lead vocalists with different styles lent to their enhanced standing among the configuration of bands within the Caribbean. Terrencia Coward, Adrian Clarke and Rupert Clarke combined to give this band the strongest vocal lineup of any Barbadian band possibly in the entire 1990s.

For The People (formerly Foreplay) was a unique experiment within Barbadian music in the 1990s. With the expansion in the number of party calypso and reggae units the formation of Foreplay out of the 1980s and 1990s groups Second Avenue and

Smooth Boyz as a rhythm and blues (R&B) act was viewed as a gamble by many pundits. Philip Forrester, its brainchild, combined his 1980s soul grooves with the fresh voices of Shane and Jermaine Forrester and the internationally sounding Toni Norville. They came up with a sound which caught the attention of critics in the Caribbean and abroad. Their two CDs, *We Got it Goin On* and *We Are Four The People??????*, epitomize the band's flair for a choric harmony driving funky bass lines and improvisations which are not overdone as they tend to be in so many R&B acts. In July of 1997, the single "Love Will Never Let You Down" featuring Peter Ram was winner of a Caribbean Star Search competition administered through Island.

Nicolas Brancker established himself as a foremost producer of calypso, soca, raggasoca and ringbang throughout the 1990s. He arranged, recorded and produced for Barbados' major artists as well as for many other artists from the region. He also made a mark when one of his jazz compositions was nominated for a Grammy Award. He produced a track for the dancehall diva Patra on the CD *Queen of Pack* and worked with the likes of Roberta Flack and Simply Red. He became a prototype for other producers who then emerged. His Chambers Studio churned out a large volume of songs. The home studio therefore took on a greater prominence within the development of music and music culture. Anthony Lowhar's Home Base and Chris Allman's Slam City were the other popular recording facilities. Other producers who emerged with their bases in self-contained small dwellings were Basil Archer, Derry Etkins, Mike Grosvenor, QSI (Promise), Darren Grant, Deepu Pajwani and School Boy, and Peter Coppin. Many artists opted for the smaller studios and cost-effective productions. Small studios were able to catch up with the output quality of much larger studios due to technological innovations. With recording boards by Tascam, Sondscraft, Peavey, Yamaha and even costlier reel-to-reel recording machines by Tascam, Sony and Philips. The movement towards full digital interface in the 1990s saw the introduction of new industry applications.

The synthesizer remained an integral and pivotal instrument throughout the 1990s. Korg's Work Station series was very popular among local live and studio musicians. These keyboards packed a lot of power and facilities. Korg's 01/W fd, for example, featured a sixteen-track sequencer with track overdubbing and tempo track editing. In addition, it offered two hundred programs, two hundred combinations, and four drum kits in its two banks, A and B, and allowed for the doubling of memory by inserting their 512K bit memory card. Other popular options in synthesizers were Korg's X and N series, Roland's D series, Yamaha's SY series, and Ensoniq's ASR and MR series. Most of these keyboards offered sequencing, sampling and recording facilities.

The computer and hard disk recording techniques became increasingly popular in shaping the recording environment. Software such as Soundblaster offered the potentiality of doing some aspects of the actual recording on the computer. The company Akai produced hardware which was designed specifically to interface with a 680x0-based Macintosh system. Some applications of recording technology did away with the computer interface and offered digital disk-based recording and editing features on one stand-alone device like Akai's DR4d hard disk recorder. Unlike the analog recording environment where hiss and "noise" are inevitable, the digital domain provided even small home-based studios with the facilities for creating high quality sounding productions. Studios therefore gave up the illusive dreams of owning high end expensive studio equipment like Tascam's ATR0-60/16 one inch-inch sixteen-track reel-to-reel recorder, or their M-700 production studio mixer with in excess of 32 buses (channels), and quad mix (dual stereo) capabilities. Small studios opted for less ostentatious yet equally effective equipment like Peavey's 16-channel Versa mixing console, and Tascam's DA-88 digital multi-track recorder was within purchasing range but still at an astounding price of 17,000 Barbadian dollars ($1 Barbadian = 50¢ US). The most revolutionary development surrounded the track recorder, the Dat recorder, and direct recording to compact disc. The introduction into the Barbadian market of the American company Alesis's Adat digital track recorder impacted the recording industry significantly. This device retailed at half the price of previous competitors and became a hot item for small studios. Alesis had also made instruments like the HR-16 drum machine more accessible to a wider range of young aspiring engineers. Track recorders were therefore being used to record the individual tracks which were then mixed down to two tracks on a Digital Audio Tape (Dat) recorder like the popular Tascam DA-30 MK11 DAT master deck. The final mix-down product could then be taken to the plant source to create the record master. Charles D. Lewis created the facility for doing a one-off CD for many artists. His equipment gave artists the option of copying a single song to a compact disk which they could then distribute to selected radio stations for air play prior to the release of the CD in large numbers.

As a result of the achievements of Barbadian artists there was an increasing acceptance of their presence in the marketplace. Barbadian artists and groups have continued to win awards in their respective categories at ceremonies held in New York, Miami and along the Eastern seaboard. But one senses that the Caribbean musical forms which are calypso oriented are still confined to a sphere of dissemination at least within the United States. Whereas Europe is a much more open market in terms of acceptance, the United States' market seems almost hostile to the inclusion of other cultural products which speak to the reality of global difference. It is ironic that present global trends point to the imperative of free trade and yet the major markets and proponents of this doctrine are firmly entrenched in a politics of exclusion. The music industry had created the neat category called "world music" as a way of defining, homogenizing and controlling the range of regional styles which demanded to be heard and could not be silenced.

But the major players within the global industry are not only money crazy moguls. There is also a larger global politics which is based on national and cultural supremacy. This politics would create a holocaust of regional others, such cultures as exist within the Caribbean. A counter argument to this suggestion will surely be that Jamaican music and Jamaican artists have been accepted beginning with Bob Marley and continuing with Shabba Ranks, BuJu Banton, Patra and Beenie Man. But the reality of the Jamaican project is that the major companies have been very skillful in redefining the cultural product of Jamaica. There is no

Jamaican artist who has risen to international status who has not been subjected to the process of assimilation. Beginning with Bob Marley, large independent and major producers have clandestinely re-configured the ideological focus of Jamaican and Caribbean products.

Too many discussions of the global impact of Caribbean music focus on the United States when there are indeed large markets as well in Europe, and Central and South America. Caribbean music administrators and planners seem to have forgotten this. In Barbados the example of Charles D. Lewis is an interesting study in this regard. He performed in Germany with the Barbadian band Harmony and eventually released a number of songs through Polygram. Songs like "Soca High" and "Soca Dance" catapulted him to the top of the various charts in Europe. This is a feat which is unequaled in the history of Barbadian music, although it might have been anticipated by Mike Grosvenor who had penned popular songs like "Long Night in Africa" in the 1980s.

At the turn of the century, the music scene in Barbados faces a range of challenges. A major hurdle which must be overcome in the immediate future is the resistance to the development of a critical tradition. The development of music in other parts of the Caribbean region has been accompanied by the expansion of critical tradition. In Jamaica, for example, there are many academic and non-academic books and writings on the music of that island. The same can be said of Trinidad where scholars like Gordon Rohlehr have intellectualized on the music and traditions of that nation. Barbados, although gaining greater respect on account of its artists, has not fostered a tradition of writings to propel this acceptance. The result of this is that Barbados lags very far behind in terms of academic discourse on its culture. The culture is therefore not as yet taken seriously in "serious" academic circles. So the industry struggles to legitimize its presence within the Caribbean and world sphere. Such a presence must be legitimized not only by the artists and performers themselves, but also by the existence of a living critical tradition which supports and itself receives support from the industry at the center. This book has been my attempt to begin to create such a critical interface for Barbadian music and culture.

GLOSSARY

aerophones. As used by Kwabena Nketia, this term refers to wind instruments.

bacchanal. Very noisy merry-making. Uproarious dance, drunken revelry.

banja. A song for dancing. In Barbados the term is used to categorize a song as being profane (said of the calypso prior to the 1980s).

banjar. Another spelling of banja.

Bumbatuk. Another name to describe the rhythm of the tuk band. The word captures the tonal properties of the tuk band's rhythm.

calabash. The fruit of the calabash tree is usually dried and used as a container. Its approximate size is slightly smaller than a soccer ball.

calypso. A popular satirical song in rhymed verse mostly associated with Trinidad, commenting on various aspects of social and political life. Mostly performed by male singers. Traditionally performed with some exptemporization directed at anyone present at the moment of performance.

calypsonian. The title given to singers of calypso.

Creole. Born in or being of the Caribbean.

cross rhythms. Refers to the complex interplay of more than one rhythmic pattern, producing a synthesis which can at times be both disconcerting and exciting. This rhythmic tendency is considered to be an integral feature of many African music styles.

dancehall. Reggae in its electronic manifestation minus the traditional message-carrying lyrics.

dub. A Caribbean rhythm produced mainly by drum and bass. A derivative of reggae associated with performers like Big Youth and U Roy. This term is used in the eastern Caribbean also to encapsulate dancehall.

duppy. In such Caribbean islands as Barbados, Belize, and Jamaica, this word refers to a threatening evil spirit, one which has been raised from the dead. A living corpse.

gospel. Used in this text to refer to a genre of music, originally a style of folk singing originally associated with evangelical revival meetings.

Hausa. Any member of the people living principally in northern Nigeria and in Niger.

ideolects. The smallest denomination of a language.

ideophone. Literally meaning "self sounding" instruments, or those upon which a sound may be produced without the addition of a stretched membrane or vibrating string or reed.

ideophonic. Said of an ideophone.

Igbo. African peoples of southeastern Nigeria. Kamau Brathwaite posits that the Barbadian slave was predominantly Igbo in origin, by way of accounting for the temperament of the African Barbadian.

jazz. A kind of music, originally improvised but now also arranged. It is characterized by syncopation, accented rhythms, dissonance and melodic variations.

Joe and Johnny. A dance performed to indigenous Caribbean song, said to have been popular in Barbados around the early 1900s.

kaiso. Another term used instead of calypso.

The Landship. A post-emancipation friendly society formed among Blacks to pool resources. They would come together to perform for a fee. Their dance routines mimicked the antics of British sailors at sea. The accompanying rhythms for their performances was contributed by the tuk band. The Landship still exists and performs in Barbados today, although it is regarded as a dying institution.

linn drum. A popular 1980s electronic drum/percussion machine. It was later manufactured by the company Akai. It was used by many Caribbean musicians as a time keeping device among other applications.

membranophones. A term used to categorize drums, usually with parchment heads.

multi-track. Refers to the process by which a song or music is constructed in the studio on the mixing board which has the facilities for recording each individual instrument on an independent channel.

mumming bands. A percussive band of St. Kitts, Jamaica. Like the tuk band, they are associated with lively holiday and festival performances.

obeah. A system of secret beliefs that incorporates the use of supernatural forces to attain or defend against evil ends.

orature. Oral literature. A term used to describe the field of non-scribal forms, prevalent in Africa and sections of the Caribbean.

over-dub. The technical process by which a recording engineer can, with the touch of a button, recall a particular musical sound or event and add another layer of sound on top of it.

penny-whistle. A musical instrument like the piccolo, played in the Barbadian tuk band.

picong. The practice among calypsonians whereby they settle or stir up debates in public through engaging in negotiated provocative exchanges during performance. Hence a picong refers to such a song which provokes a response on account of its use of biting satire or wit.

polyrhythms. Same as cross rhythms.

pop-spouge. I use this definition to describe a number of progressive musical practices which were being experimented with during the 1970s in Barbados. In particular I refer to the very polished recorded tracks by the likes of Mickey D's "Bet Yuh Life;" The Sand Pebbles' "Another Dream;" Lunar 7's "Another Try;" Super 8's "Come Back Girl;" and The Bimshire Boys' "Simple Song."

raggasoca. A fusion of the popular electronically driven reggae style called ragga (associated with artists like Shakademus and Pliers) and the calypso dance music, soca.

riffs. A repeated musical phrase used especially as a background as a basic theme within a musical composition.

rim shot. Refers to the metal rim of the snare drum and the sound produced when this metal section is struck.

ringbang. A 1990s musical phenomenon. Performed predominantly by Barbadian artists. For this reason many lay persons consider it to be a

Barbadian style. This name was given to a musical style by the international recording artist Eddy Grant. This style privileges the drums above (or instead of) other instruments. Presently, this style has its greatest application in the soca and calypso domain. Whereas a strict calypso may highlight the horns, a ringbang calypso would strip the arrangement down to drum and bass instruments.

ringbang säf or **ringbang soft.** The quieter, slower application of ringbang.

rock steady. A type of music in Jamaica which developed after ska and later gave way to reggae. Rock steady was characterized by a steady rhythm and noticeable off-beat.

ruk-a-tuk. Like Bumbatuk, this term also describes the music of the tuk band.

snare shot. The sound produced by striking the snare drum of a percussive band like the tuk band or the standard drum set.

soca. A dance-oriented derivative of calypso evolving around the mid 1970s and coming into acceptance and popularity by the middle of the 1980s.

spouge. A musical rhythm having its origins in Barbados in the late 1960s. Its creator is the late Jackie Opel. A musical style which sits somewhere between calypso and reggae in its overall resultant rhythm. Between 1970 and 1975 there was a phenomenal rise in record productions in Barbados. This was directly attributed to spouge. In the early 1970s, the foot drum and the rim shot were pivotal in affecting the recurrent off-beat of spouge. The cow bell and the rhythm guitarist's strumming up and down on the plectrum complete the list of important instruments of 1970s spouge. Today other musical instruments are utilized in its performance.

spouge tot. A popular word used to rename the cow bell. It was so called because of its integral function in the spouge combo. This sound was also considered to be an indispensable component of spouge.

steel. The timpani.

susu. A friendly saving scheme where each member contributes weekly or monthly and on a rotating basis each one receives a total amount. Also called the "meeting turn."

synclavier. A 1980s piano or synthesizer noted for its rich tones. But also once considered an expensive piece of equipment.

toms. Another name for the drums which comprise the drum set.

Top-40. A term used to describe the major pop styles heard on United States chart shows with the likes of Casey Casem.

tuk. The rhythm or music of the tuk band.

tuk band. An indigenous troupe of musicians who first came together on the sugar plantation to provide music for festivities. Since African instruments were banned in Barbados from early in its history, these musicians substituted European snare, bass and kettle drums, but still maintained the polyrhythmic cross rhythms of their "traditional" African cultures. These bands are still functioning today in Barbados, and as with the Landship, there are conscious attempts to sustain these entities.

up-tempo. Used to describe the lively, fast-paced rhythms of some Caribbean music forms like soca and ringbang.

world beat. A term coined by the international music industry in the West, in popular use in the 1980s. It describes the wide range of regional "ethnic" and exotic music which were sought after and flirted with by some major recording companies in the middle and late 1980s.

SELECTED DISCOGRAPHY
OF BARBADIAN MUSIC

Adisa. *Conscious*. AFA Music. REM 003 (1993).

Adonijah. *Amandla!* Wirl. WK 279 (1988).

Alleyne, Mike. *Alien In The Street*. AirSign. AAOOl (1989).

Alleyne, Wendy. *Standby Love. Let it Show. I Have a Thing About You.*

Barbados Festival Choir. *Folk Songs of Barbados*. Wirl W 1006 (1964).

Bimshire Boys. *Simple Song.*

Blue Rhythm Combo. *Do You Like Spouge Music. Knock on Wood. Lonesome Me.*

Brathwaite, Edward Kamau. *Rights of Passage*. Argo PLP 111011 (1969). *Masks.* Argo PLP 1183 (1972). *Islands*. Argo PLP 11844/5 (1973).

Brown, Bert. *Bajan Heat*. ICE 005 (1992).

Bumba. *Fortune Teller*. Wirl WK404 (1993).

Campbell, Desmond. *Calypso Variations*. Wirl DKC 001 (1987). An innovative album ahead of its time. Kalabash utilizes such instruments as the Yamaha DX7, Yamaha TX 816, SCI Prophet, Linn 2000, Korg EX800, and the Commodore SX-64 computer. Features such songs as "Me Island," "Mr. DJ," "Play Calypso," "Happy Song," and "We Jumping."

Caribbean Rhythms. *The Friendship*. Wirl W/011 (1987).

Checkmates. *Dream. I'm Always Thinking of You. Talking 'Bout Music.* (1977).

Chocolate Affair. *Jam!* Wirl CA-K 004 (1988). *Fun Time*. Wirl CA 001 (1987).

Christ Church Parish Church. Wirl W cas 227.

Classic. *Full Blast*. Wirl JT-K009 (1988).

Clay, Cassius. *Sweeter Than a Snow Cone.*

Cockroach. *On My Feet Again*. Mahogany Bird Records MBK 002. *Stop De Crime*. MBK 001.

Cockspur 5 Star Steel Orchestra. *Barbados Vol. 1*. Wirl cas W 232. *Barbados Vol. 2*. K257. *Barbados Vol. 3*. Wirl Wk 287.

Comforters, Gospel. *Changing World*. RED 0024 (1992). *Jesus is The Rock*. Wirl 0017. *Try Jesus*. RED 0020 (1987).

Draytons Two. *Blueberry Hill. The Lion Sleeps Tonight. Written Down. Emalie. Reflections of My Life. G.O Go. Gimme Back Me Dollar. People Get Up. Play That Spouge Music. Can't Keep a Good Man Down.* Emily A&B Music (1987).

Escorts. *Sylvia's Mother. Cream Puff. Who Ain't Looking Good.*
Exodus. *Never Had a Love.* Wirl B1075 (1989).

Fantastics. *Meet The Fabulous Fantastics.* LSC 010 (1990).
Farrell, I. *Earth Spirit.* FARCIA FF004 (1994). *21 and Moving On.* FARCIA FAR002 (1987). *Jamming.* FAR003 (1991).
Fingall, Mac. *A Go Wine.* Bayfield BF028 (1991). *Men Wake Up.* Bayfield BF 036 (1993). *What Is Soca.* Bayfield BF K 038 (1994). *Unocep.* Bayfield BF 032 (1992).
Flatbush. *Poor Man's Son.*

Gabby. *Never Me Again.* (1969). *Licks Like Fire/Needles and Pins.* Wirl SH 001 (1979). *Burn Mr Hardin.* Wirl (1979). *One In The Eye.* ICE BGI 1001 (1986). *The Right Mix.* ICE BGI (1987). *The Right Super Mix.* ICE BGI (1987). *The Right Mix Vol. 2.* ICE BGI (1988). *Across The Board.* ICE BGI 1010 (1989). *Illegal Tender.* ICE BGI (1990). *Large And In Charge.* ICE BGI 002 (1992). *500 Blue.* ICE BGI 003 (1992).
Grazette, Tony. *Bring Back de Spouge.* (1987).
Grovesnor, Mike. *It's My Life.* Wirl W 183 (1983). *Mike Grovesnor's Best.* Wirl WK 400 (1993).
Grynner. *The Road March King.* ICE 89 (1989).

Hilltones. *Let That Someone Be Me.*
Hot Gossip. *Live.* Produced by Hot Gossip for Red Pepper Records.
Hunte, David. *The Petition.* W998 (1986).

Iley, Ras. *High Riding.* Wirl WK 320. *King Of The Stage.* Wirl WK 395.
Ivory. *Mini Bus Fus.* Tusk 005 (1990). *Print Out.* cass TL -002. (1984). *Love Just a Word.* TUSK009 (1989). *Dangerous Beat.* TUSK007 (1986).

Jesse James. *Dub is the Force*, Volcano (1987). *Splish Splash*, WIRL W1048 (1988).

King, John. *Awesome*. Wirl no cat. (1988). *Psyched*. Wirl WK437 (1994). Krosfyah. *Utimate Party*. Wirl WK 443 (1994).

Lady Ann (with Bing Bong). *Lady Ann (with Bing Bong)*. Sounds Gud SG 041 (1994).
Lisle. *My Charming Little Island Home*. Wirl cass W 095 (1984).
Love Me or Leave Me. Hey Mr. Blues.
Lunar Seven. *All I Need is Another Try? Baby I Can Make it By Myself. Here l Am Baby.*

Madd. *Cocktails*. Madd 004 (1989). *Greatest Hits*. Madd 006 (1991). *I Like It Badd*. Madd K 001. (1988). *Ramifications*. Madd 005 (1990). *Slippery When Wet*. Madd 008 (1993). *Tuh Jenkins And Back*. Wirl no cat. Contains songs like "Big Bungalow" and "Push."
Malcolm X, DJ. *Various Artists Remixed*. Wirl WK447 (1994).
Merrymen. *Barbados Memories*. Merry Disc MM5 1033 (1984). *Calypso and Island Songs*. Merry Disc MM 1046 (1991). *Come To My Island*. Merry Disc MM5 1038 (1984). *Hot Hot Soca*. Merry Disc MMS 1045 (1989). *Island Treasure*. Merry Disc MM5 1044 (1988). *Merrymen Live in Ontario Place*. Merry Disc MM 1039 (1988). *Party Animal*. Merry Disc MM5 1043 (1988). *Sugar Jam*. Merry Disc M5 1036. *Sweet Fuh Days*. Merry Disc MM CD 1046. *Tropical Wave*. Merry Disc MM5 1042 (1985).
Mickey D. *Bet Yuh Life I Do.*
Niles, Joseph. *Accept Jesus*. RED 28 (1995). *Christmas Bells*. RED-0014 (1986). *Climbing Up The Mountain*. (with the Consolers) RED 0001 (1984). *Ever Shall It Be*. RED 0013 (1986). *Feast of Belshazzar*. RED 0016 (1985). *Go On To Glory Vol. l*. RED 0026 (1992). *Go On To Glory Vol. 2*. RED 26 (1993). *Go To The Lord In Prayer*. RED 027 (1993). *Gospel Ship*. (with the Consolers) RED 0002. *Heaven" Joy Awaits*. Redemption RED 0023 (1991). *Keep On Praying*. (with the Consolers) RED 007 (1987). *Lead Me Gently*. RED 00021. *Look On The Brighter Side*. RED 0022 (1989). *Old Time Favourites*. (with the Consolers) RED CASS 0006 (1984). *On the Jericho Road*. (with the Consolers) RED 0009 (1987). *Peace Be Still*. RED 0015 (1984). *Power in the Blood*. RED 0018 (1990). *Royal Telephone*. RED 0004 (1974). *Swing Down Chariot*. RED cass 0011

(1985). *This Train*. Wirl WK013 (1990). *Through It All: Twenty Five Years Of Joseph Niles*. RED 0019 (1995).
Njeri and Solar Energy. *Panga-Lang*, DS777 (1988).

Opel, Jackie. *Worrell's Captaincy/T.V in Jamaica*. Island JU 512 (196?). *Jackie Opel The Memorable*. Wirl W 015 (1984).
Organisation. *Bye Bye Love. Help Me Love.*

Pompey. *After Dark*. Wirl no cat. (1987). *Young Ting*. Wirl no cat. (1988). Project H&T. *Halleluijah Beat*. PROJ 001 (1990).
Promise. *Crucified*. PRO 003 (1987). *Safari Search*. Wirl cass K 225 (1984).
Pure Gold. *Love*, Wirl B1032 (1987).
Put Your Hand On De Bumper. CRS 0021 (1994). *Ragga Soca Dancehall Hits*. Wirl WK 456 (1994). Features Black Pawn, Ras Iley, Daddy Mark, Troubadours, DJ Grandmaster, John King, Krosfyah, and Adonijah. *Recollections*, Wirl WK269 (1990). Features Jackie Opel, The Draytons, Rudy Boyce, Richard Stoute, The Revelations, Wendy Alleyne, The Dynamics, June Knight, Go Flook Richards and The Troubadours, Lunar 7, Ches Haynes, Fern Trail and The Fantastics, The Opels, Solid Senders, Mickey Dee, and The Merry Boys featuring Frank Mosbaugh. *Soca By Four*. Wirl. WK 397. *Soca Spirit*. Wirl WK 398. Features Black Pawn and David Hunte and the songs "Soca Dancehall," "Rude Boy Warning," "Do It" and "Questions." *Songs of Redemption*. RED 003 (1987). Features Margreta Marshall's "Good News" and "I Have Salvation"; Ann Riley's "Just A Closer Walk" and "He Touched Me"; Peter Clarke's "A Beautiful Life"; Darnel Straker's "He Searched For Me"; Gospel Comforters' "Lonesome Valley" and "Jesus Hold To Me"; and Joseph Niles' "It's No Secret" and "How Can I Forget." These are all backed by The Consolers. *Super Crop Over Vol.5*. Wirl WK 368 (1992). *Super Crop Over Vol.6*. Wirl WK 396 (1993). *Super Crop Over Party*. Wirl WK 280 (1988). *Super Gospel Live 1986 Vol. 1*. no cat. NS (1986). *Vacation Time-Barbados*. Wirl WK 379 (1993). Features Caribbean Rhythms, Sygnacha, Island Fever, Second Avenue, Splashband, Sylkk, and The Merrymen. *Victory: Choir Festival, 1986*. MSC K0003 (1987).

R.P.B. *Happiness*. Bayfield BF 035 (1993). *Hitting De Front*. Bayfield BF K 037 (1994).
Revelations. *Don't Want No Young Girls*.

Roberts, Howard. *A Lovely Way to Spend an Evening*. Wirl WK 356. *Standards from the Forties*. Wirl WK 329.

Sandpebbles. *Someone Will Bring Another Dream*. (1973). *Put on Your Wings and Fly?? Someday My Love. If Sandra Want to Wine.*

Saturn. *Off My Mind*, MaxiMusic MM007 (1986).

Second Avenue. *The Time is Right*, SA002 (1988).

Serenader. *Party Menu*. Wirl WK 430 (1994). *Rough And Tough*. Wirl no cat. (1988).

Side One. *Don't Wanna Be Lonely*, Cari-Jam CJ002 (1989).

Silvertones. *I'm Yours Lord*. American Artists AA 1678 CS (1989).

Solid Senders. *So Nice To Be With You.*

Spice. *Camouflage*. CRS CRS-T 007 (1993). *Dance Across The Seas*. Wirl WK 313 (1990). *Different World*. Wirl Wk 293. *The First Decade*. CRS CD 011. *The First Fifteen*. Wk 340 (1991). Contains "Sad Love," "Always On My Mind," "Nobody Can Hurt Me Now," and "The Itch." *Form and Fashion*. Freedom SP005 (1985). Contains "Always On My Mind" and "Sad Love." *In De Congaline*. Irie Music SP 013 (1988). *World Dance*. CRST003 (1992).

Splashband. *Champion Sound*. Wirl SB-K 002 (1993). *The Game of life*. [as Sunsplash] Wirl W 324 (1990). Contains "When You're Not Around," "Soca Lambada," "Free," "I Am The One," and "The Budget." Lead vocalist is Jeoffrey Cordle. *X-Amonkomusic*. Splashband Music SP X-AK 001 (1991). *Riddim-A-Ton*, CRS 0028 (1995).

Square One. *Eat Drink And Be Merry*. Bayfield no cat. (1989). Contains "JumpJump," "Bad," and "Happy Fuh Days." *Special*. ICE 004/94.

St. Michael's Cathedral Choir. *St. Michael's Cathedral Choirin Boston*. Wirl K/K 245 (1986). *St. Michael's Cathedral Choir in London*. Wirl cass. W 021.

Stewart, Shirley. *Don't Rain on My Parade*, Walsturn (1986).

Stoute, Richard. *Greatest Hits*. Wirl W157. *Teen Talent*. Wirl W 410 (1993). *Your Vehicle. Any Day Now.*

Straker, Emile. *Bubbling Soca*. Wirl W 1086 (1989).

Super Eight. *Come Back Girl.*

Sygnacha. *Move Yuh Mass*. (1993).

Syndicate. *Fun In The Sun*. DMS 001 (1992).

Tappin, Arturo. *Strictly Roots Jazz*. SAX roots/BMI SXR 001.

Tropical Islanders. *Do It Your Own Way*. MMSK 013.

Troubadoures. *Bouncing*. Wirl WK 427 (1994). *Find A Way*. Wirl MMS 018 (1990). Contains "Faith," "Share Your Love," "Woman In Jail" and "You Got Me." *De Ting Sweet*.WirlWK387 (1993).

Twentieth Anniversary Party: Live at The Warehouse. Contains "Dangerous Beat."

Tyrone and Exotic Steel Orchestra. *Steel Barbados Style*. Wirl cass. W 096.

Tyrone and the Clouds. *Steel Band and Calypso*. Merry Disc CAV 51035.

Various Artists. *The Best of Barbados*. Wirl (1989) no cat. *The Best of Caribbean Christian Artists*. Network CCAN 001 (1993). *Caribbean House Party 2*. Wirl WK 386 (1993). Features Speedy, Sly-La-RY, Ian Greaves, and the I Crew. *Crop Over Calypso Jump-up Mix. Vol.2*. Wirl WK 284 (1988). *Crop Over Calypso Soca Session Vol. 4*. Wirl WK 407. *Crop Over Soca (Session Mix) Vol.5*. Wirl W 446 (1994). *De Congaline*. CRS CT 018 (1994). *Down De Road: Barbados Crop Over Hits*. Wirl WK-285 (1988). *Fire One For De Road*. CRSLP 21 (l994). *Four Is A Party*. Wirl WK 428 (1994). Features Observer, Classic, and Structure. *Harmony: Memories of Choir Festival 1985 Vol.1*. MSC no cat. (1985). *On Fire: Memories of Choir Festival*. 1990. MSC K006. *Heart Warming Gospel Songs*. RED 0010. Features Redeemed Gospel Band, Gospel Comforters, Love Circle, and Joseph Niles. *Jump Up Party*. Wirl WK 432 (1994). Features Bumba, Stalker, and Hawk. *Kadooment Crop Over Party*. Wirl WCD 441-2. *Kadooment Wuk-Up Jam!* Wirl WCD 408.

Ward, Piercy. *Swaying Palms and Changing Moods*. Wirl PW 3000.

Wesley Singers of Barbados. *Great Hymns of Methodism*. Wirl cas-no cat. (1985).

Xenon. *Don't Touch De Crack*, Wirl B1025 (1987).

Zoe. *Jesus I Believe in You*. WK 357 (1992).

BIBLIOGRAPHY

Abraham, Kinfe. *From Race to Race.* (London: Grassroots Publisher, 1982).

Abraham, Roger. *The Man of Words in the West Indies.* (Baltimore: Johns Hopkins University Press, 1983).

—. "A Performance Centered Approach to Gossip." *Man 5.* (1970) 290-301.

African Folklore in the New World. Edited by Daniel Crowley. (Austin: University of Texas Press, 1977).

Afro-American Anthropology: Contemporary Perspectives. Edited by John Szwed and Norman Whitten. (New York: Free Press, 1970).

Agawu, Kofi. "Refreshing African Music." *Critical Inquiry.* Vol.18, No. 2 (1992) 245-266.

Alexander, J. *Transatlantic Sketches.* Vol. 1 (London, 1833).

Alleyne, Mervyn. "A Linguistic Perspective on the Caribbean." *Caribbean Contours.* Edited by Mintz. 155-179.

—. *Contemporary Afro-American.* (Ann Arbour: Karoma, 1980).

—. *Introduction to Theoretical Orientations in Creole Studies.* Edited by Valdman. 1-17.

—. "Acculturation and the Cultural Matrix." *Pidginization.* Edited by Hymes. 169-184.

Alleyne, Warren. *The Barbados-Carolina Connection.* (London: McMillan Caribbean Ltd., 1988).

Allsopp, Richard. "How Does the Creole Lexicon Expand." *Theoretical Orientations.* Edited by Valdman. 89-107.

—. "The Lexicography of Creolized English as a Cultural Integrator in the Caribbean." *Carib.* No. 3 (1983) 1-8.

Anyidoho, Kofi. "Oral Poetics and Traditions of Verbal Art in Africa." Ph.D dissertation. (University of Texas at Austin: Microfilms Intl., 1983).

Apte, Mahadev. *Humor and Laughter: An Anthropological Approach*. (Ithaca: Cornell University Press, 1985).

Arant, Patricia. "Formulaic Studies and The Russian Bylina." *Indiana Slavic Studies*. 4 (1967) 8-41.

Armstrong, Robert. "The Collection of Oral Tradition in Africa." *African Notes*. Vol. 5, No. 2 (January 1969) 12-16.

Asein, S. "The Protest Tradition in West Indian Poetry from George Campbell to Martin Carter." *Jamaica Journal*. Vol. 6, No. 2 (June 1972) 40-45.

Ashcroft, Bill, et al. *The Empire Writes Back*. (London: Routledge, 1989).

Aspects of the Blues. Edited by Paul Oliver. (New York: Oak Publications, 1970).

Auike, Macpherson. "Code Switching as a Strategic Device." *Critical Theory*. Edited by Emenyonu. 234-247.

Babalola, A. "The Characteristic Features of Outer Form in Yoruba Ijala Chants." *Odu*. Vol. 1, No. 1 & 2 (1964-5):5-11.

Baker, Houston. *Blues, Ideology and AfroAmerican Literature. A Vernacular Theory*. (Chicago: University of Chicago Press, 1984).

Bame, Kwabena. *Come to Laugh: African Traditional Theatre in Ghana*. (New York: Lilian Barber Press Inc., 1985).

Baraka, Amiri. *Daggers and Javelins: Essays 1974-1979*. (New York: Quill, 1984).

Barber, Karin. *I Could Speak Until Tomorrow*. (London: Edingburgh University Press, 1991).

Baudet, Martha. "Identifying the African Grammatical Base of the Caribbean Creoles: A Topological Approach." *Historicity and Variation*. Edited by Highfield. 104-116.

Bebey, Francis. *African Music: A People's Art*. (New York: Lawrence Hill and Co., 1975).

Bennett, Susan. *Theatre Audiences: A Theory of Production*. (London: Routledge, 1990).

Benson, Larry. "The Literary Character of Anglo-Saxon Formulaic Poetry." *Modern Language Association*. 81 (1966) 334.

Best, Curwen. "Caribbean Music and the Politics of Confinement." *People Power Progress*. Edited by Glyne Griffith.

—. "Co-related Aspects of Technique in Caribbean Oral and Written Verse." *The Comic Vision in West Indian Literature*. Edited by Roydon Salick. (Port of Spain: Department of English, 1993).

—. "Text Tradition Technology Crossover and Caribbean Popular Culture." *Pressures of the Text.* Edited by Stewart Brown. (Birmingham: C.W.A.S, 1995).

Bickerton, Derek. *Dynamics of a Creole System.* (London: Cambridge University Press, 1975).

—. *Roots to Language.* (AnnArbor: Karoma Publishers Inc., 1981).

Bilby, Kenneth. "The Caribbean as a Musical Region." *Caribbean Contours.* Edited by Mintz. 180-215.

—. "Caribbean Crucible." *Repercussions: A Celebration of African AmericanMusic.* Edited by Geoffrey Haydon et al. 70-89.

Black Music in Britain: Essays on the Afro-Asian Contribution to Popular Music. Edited by Paul Oliver. (Milton Keynes: Open University Press, 1990).

Brathwaite, Edward Kamau. *The Arrivants: A New World Trilogy.* (London: Oxford University Press, 1973).

—. "Bruce St John and the Bajan Oral Tradition." *Public Lecture.* (Bridgetown, 1990).

—. "Caliban's Garden." *Wasafiri.* No. 16 (Autumn 1992) 2-6.

—. "Caribbean Women During the Period of Slavery." *Caribbean Contact.* (June 1984) 13.

—. "Commentary on Afro-American Slave Culture." *Roots and Branches.* Edited by Michael Craton. 153-154.

—. *Contradictory Omens: Culture and Diversity in Integration in the Caribbean.* (Mona: Savacou Publications, 1974).

—. *History of the Voice.* (London: New Beacon Books, 1984).

—. "Jazz and the West Indian Novel." *BIM* 44-46 (January 1967-June 1968):275-284; 39-51; 115-126.

—. "The Mighty Sparrow-Slinger Francisco." *The New Voices.* Vol. 20, Nos. 39/40 (March-Sept 1992) 110-128.

—. *Mother Poem.* (Oxford: Oxford University Press, 1977).

—. "The Poet: His Place in Bajan Culture." XIIth Sir Winston Scott Memorial Lecture. (December 4, 1987).

—. *Sun Poem.* (Oxford: Oxford University Press, 1982).

—. *X/Self.* (Oxford: Oxford University Press, 1987).

Brother Resistance. *Rapso Explosion.* (London: Karia Press, 1986).

Brown, Lloyd. *West Indian Poetry.* (Boston: Twayne Publishers, 1978).

Burrowes, Audrey. "Barbadian Creole: A Note on its Social History and Structure." *Studies in Caribbean Language.* Edited by Carrington. 38-45.

Callender, Timothy. *The Elements of Art*. (St Michael: Privately published, 1977).

Campbell, Deanna, et al. *Music at the Margins: Popular Music and Global Cultural Diversity*. (Newbury Park: Sage Publications, 1991).

Carnival! Edited by Thomas Sebeok. (Berlin: Mouton Publishers, 1984).

Carrington, Lawrence. *Studies in Caribbean Language*. (Cave Hill: U.W.I. School of Education, 1983).

Cashmore, E. *Rastaman*. (London: Unwin Paperbacks, 1983).

Cassidy, Frederic. "Barbadian Creole." Presented at the Conference of the Society for Caribbean Linguists (Surinam, 1982).

Chaim, Daphna. *Distance in the Theatre: The Aesthetics of Audience Response*. (Ann Arbor: UMI Research Press, 1984).

Charney, Maurice. *Comedy High and Low*. (New York: Oxford University Press, 1978).

Chernoff, John. *African Rhythm and African Sensibility*. (Chicago: University of Chicago Press, 1979).

Collymore, Frank. *Notes for a Glossary of Words and Phrases of Barbadian Dialect*. (Bridgetown: Advocate Company, 1965).

Contemporary Poets of the English Language. Edited by Rosalie Murphy. (London: St James Press, 1970).

Cook, Harold. *Shaker Music: A Manifestation of American Folk Music*. (New Jersey: Associated University Press, 1973).

Cordwell, J. "Continuity and Change in African Cultures." *Artist and Audience*. Edited by Richard Priebe and Thomas Hale. (Washington: Three Continents Press, 1979) 22-40.

Corrigan, R. *Comedy: Meaning and Form*. (New York: Harper and Row, 1981).

Courlander, Harold. *Negro Folk Music, USA*. (New York: Columbia University Press, 1963).

Craig, Dennis. "Education and Creole English in the West Indies: Some Sociolinguistic Factors." *Pidginization and Creolization of Language*. Edited by Hymes. 371-389.

Craton, Michael. *Testing the Chains: Resistance to Slavery in the British West Indies*. (Ithaca: Cornell University Press, 1982).

Critical Essays on Ezra Pound. Edited by Walter Sutton. (New Jersey: Prentice Hall Inc., 1963).

Critical Theory and Oral Literature. Edited by Ernest Emenyonu. (Ibadan: Heinemann, 1987).

Cross Rhythms: Papers on African Folklore. Edited by Anyidoho. (Indiana: The Trickster Press, 1983).

Cudjoe, Selwyn. *Resistance and Caribbean Literature.* (Ohio: Chicago University Press, 1980).

Dalphinis, Morgan. *Caribbean and African Languages.* (London: Karia Press, 1985).

De Leon, Raphael. *Calypso From France to Trinidad.* (Port of Spain: General Printers, 1988).

Devonish, Hubert. "Creole Languages and the Process of Socio-Economic Domination in the Caribbean." *Carib.* No. 3 (1983) 52-66.

—. *Language and Liberation: Creole Language Politics in the Caribbean.* (London: Karia Press, 1986).

Dickson, William. *Letters on Slavery.* (London: J. Phillips, 1789).

Drewett, Peter. *Prehistoric Barbados.* (London: University College London, 1991).

Dundes, Alan. *Interpreting Folklore.* (Bloomington: Indiana University Press, 1980).

Dyott, William. *Dyott's Diary 1781-1845.* (London, 1907).

Early Music Discography: From Plainsongs to the Songs of Bach. Vols. 1 and 2. Edited by Trevor Croucher. (London: Library Association Publishing, 1981).

Easthope, Anthony. *Literary Into Cultural Studies.* (London: Routledge, 1991).

Eco, Umberto. "The Frames of Comic Freedom." *Carnival!* Edited by Thomas A. Sebeok. 1-8.

—. *The Role of the Reader.* (Bloomington: Indiana University Press, 1979).

Edwards, Brian. *The History, Civil and Commercial of the British Colonies in the West Indies.* (Dublin, 1793).

Edwards, Victor, et al. *Oral Cultures Past and Present.* (Massachusetts: Basil Blackwell, 1990).

Elder, Jacob. "Evolution of the Traditional Calypso of Trinidad and Tobago: A Socio-Historical Analysis of Song Change." Ph.D Thesis (Ann Arbor, Michigan, 1966).

Elliot, Robert. *The Power of Satire.* (Princeton: Princeton University Press, 1960).

Ellis, Guy. "Remembering the Terra." *Lucian Kaiso.* No. 1 (Souvenir Magazine, February 1990).

Ellison, Mary. *Extensions of the Blues.* (London: John Calder, 1989).

Emenyonu, Ernest. *Black Culture and Black Consciousness in Literature*. (Ibadan: Heinemann, 1987).

Emery, Lynne. *Black Dance From 1619 to Today*. (London: Princeton Books, 1988).

Epstein, Dena. *Sinful Tunes and Spirituals*. (Urbana: University of Illinois Press, 1977).

Essays on Music and History in Africa. Edited by K.P. Wachsmann. (Evanston: Northwestern University Press, 1971).

Essays on the Visual and Verbal Arts. Edited by June Helm. (Seattle: University of Washington Press, 1967).

Feinberg, Leonard. *Introduction to Satire*. (Iowa: Iowa State University Press, 1967).

—. *Blues from the Delta*. London: Studio Vista, 1970.

Finnegan, Ruth. *Oral Traditions and the Verbal Arts*. (London: Routledge, 1992).

—. "Communication and Technology." *Language and Communications*. 9 (1989) 107-127.

—. *Oral Literature in Africa*. (London: Oxford University Press, 1970).

Folk Music and Modern Sound. Edited by William Ferris and Mary Hurt. (Mississippi: University Press of Mississippi, 1982).

Folklore and Folklife: An Introduction. Edited by Richard Dorson. (Chicago: University of Chicago, 1972).

Franklyn, Gilbert. *A Reply to R. B .Nicholls*. (London, 1790).

Frith, Simon. "Literary Studies as Cultural Studies." *Critical Quarterly*. Vol. 34, No. 1 (1992) 3-24.

—. *Sound Effects: Youth, Leisure, and the Politics of Rock and Roll*. (New York: Pantheon, 1981).

Galenson, David. *Traders, Planters and Slaves: Market Behaviour in Early English America*. (Cambridge: Cambridge University Press, 1986).

Ganyi, Mowang. "Performance Composition in Bakon Song Texts: A View of the Parry-Lord Oral Formulaic Theory." *Critical Theory and Oral Literature*. Edited by Ernest Emenyonu. 144-158.

Hall, Robert. *Acts Passed in the Island of Barbados 1643-1762*. (London, 1964).

Hall, Stuart. "Culture, Media and the 'Ideological Effect.'" *Mass Communication and Society*. Edited by Curran. 315-348.

Hammersly, Martyn. *Reading Ethnographic Research: A Critical Reader.* (London: Longman, 1990).

—. *What's Wrong With Ethnography.* (London: Routledge, 1992).

Hancock, Ian. "Gullah and Barbadian Origins and Relationships." Presented at the International Conference on Pidgins and Creoles (1975).

Handler, Jerome. "Aspects of Slave Life in Barbados' Music and its Cultural Context." *Caribbean Studies.* Vol. 11 (1972) 5-46.

—. *Plantation Slavery in Barbados: An Archeological and Historical Investigation.* (Cambridge: Harvard University Press, 1978).

Hare, Maud Cuney. *Negro Musicians and their Music.* (Washington: Associated Publishers, 1936).

Harlow, Barbara. *Resistance Literature.* (New York: Methuen, 1987).

Harlow, Vincent. *A History of Barbados 1625-1685.* (Oxford: Clarendon Press, 1926).

Henderson, Stephen. "Saturation: Progress Report on a Theory of Black Poetry." *Black World.* 24 (1975) 14.

Henige, David. *The Chronology of Oral Tradition: Quest for a Chimera.* (Oxford: Clarendon Press, 1974).

Hennessey, Thomas. "From Jazz to Swing: Black Jazz Musicians and their Music 1917-1935." Ph.D dissertation (Northwestern University, 1973).

Herndon, M. *Field Manual for Ethnomusicology.* (Norwood: Norwood Editions, 1983).

Highfield, Arnold. *Theoretical Orientations in Creole Studies.* (New York: Academia Press, 1980).

Hill, Errol. "The Trinidad Carnival: Cultural Change and Synthesis." *Cultures.* Vol. 3, No. 11 (France, 1976) 54-85.

Hilton, Julian. *New Directions in Theatre Performance.* (Hampshire: McMillan, 1987).

Hippolyte, Kendal. "Judging Calypso." *Lucian Kaiso.* (1990) 28-29, 33.

Hirsch, P. *The Structure of the Popular Music Industry.* (Michigan: Ann Arbor, 1970).

Ho Lung, Richard. "Sinner. Fame Priest Raps on God and Culture." *Caribbean Contact* Vol. 2 No. 9 (December 1974) 19.

Holland, Norman. *Laughter: A Psychology of Humor.* (Ithaca: Cornell University Press, 1982).

Holm, John. *Pidgins and Creoles. Vol. 2.* (Cambridge: Cambridge University Press, 1989).

Homan, Roger. *The Ethics of Social Research.* (London: Longman, 1991).

Hood, M. *The Ethnomusicologist.* (Ohio: Kent State University, 1982).

Howard-Malverde, Rasaleen. "Storytelling Strategies in Quechua Narrative Performance." *Journal of Latin American Lore.* Vol.15 No.1 (Summer 1989) 3-68.

Hughes, G. *The Natural History of Barbados.* (New York: Arno Press, 1972).

Hutchinson, Thomas. *Impressions of Western Africa.* (London: Frank Cass, 1858).

"Interpreting Oriki as History and as Literature." *Discourse and Its Disguises: The Interpretation of African Oral Texts.* Edited by Karin Barber. (Center of West African Studies: University of Birmingham, 1989) 13-24.

Ismond, Patricia. "Walcott Versus Brathwaite." *Caribbean Quarterly.* Vol. 17 Nos. 3 & 4 (September-December 1971) 54-71.

Issacharoff, Michael, et al. *Performing Texts.* (Philadelphia: University of Pennsylvania Press, 1988).

Jacobs, Arthur. *The New Penguin Dictionary of Music.* (Harmondsworth: Penguin Books Ltd., 1977).

Jobson, Richard. *The Golden Trade.* (London: N. Okes, 1623).

Jones, A.M. *Studies in African Music.* (Oxford: Oxford University Press, 1959).

Jones, LeRoi. *Black Music.* (New York: William Morrow Co. Inc., 1968).

—. *Blues People.* (New York: William Morrow Co. Inc., 1963).

Julien, Eileen. *African Novels and the Question of Orality.* (Bloomington: Indiana University Press, 1992).

Karpeles, Maud. *English Folksong.* (Oxford: Oxford University Press, 1987).

Kemp, Sandra. "Performing Cultural Studies." *Critical Quarterly.* Vol. 34 No. 1 (1992) 36-49.

Kershaw, Baz. *The Politics of Performance: Radical Theatre as Cultural Intervention.* (London: Routledge, 1992).

Kingman, Daniel. *American Music: A Panorama.* (NewYork: Scribner Books, 1979).

Kiwanuka, M. "African Pre-Colonial History: A Challenge to the Historian's Craft." *Afrika Zamani: Review of African History.* Nos. 6 & 7 (December 1977) 23-35.

Klotman, P. "BlackMusic." *Reflections on Afro-American Music.* Edited by Dominique de Lerma. (Kent: State University Press, 1973) 59-108.

Le Page, Robert. "Dialect in West Indian Literature." *Critics on Caribbean Literature*. Edited by Baugh. 82-98.

Levine, Lawrence. *Black Culture and Black Consciousness*. (New York: Oxford University Press, 1977).

Ligon, Richard. *A True and Exact History of the Island of Barbados*. (London, 1673).

Lomax, Alan. *The Folk Song of North America*. (New York: Doubleday and Co. Inc., 1960).

—. *Folk Song Style and Culture*. (New Brunswick: Transaction Books, 1968).

Lombardo, Patricia. "Cultural Studies and Interdisciplinarity." *Critical Quarterly*. Vol. 34 No. 3 (Autumn 1992) 3-10.

Lord, Albert. *The Singer of Tales*. (Cambridge: Massachusetts, 1960).

McCabe, Colin. "Cultural Studies and English." *Critical Quarterly*. Vol. 34 No. 3 (Autumn 1992) 25-34.

McGhee, Paul, et al. *Handbook of Humor Research*. (New York: Springer—Verlag, 1983).

Makinson, David. *Barbados: A Study of North-American-West Indian Relations 1759-1789*. (London: Mouton and Co., 1965).

Malone, Bill. *Southern Music. American Music*. (Lexington: University Press of Kentucky, 1979).

Marre Jeremy. *Beats of the Heart: Popular Music of the World*. (London: Pluto Press, 1985).

Marshall, Trevor. "History and Evolution of Calypso in Barbados." (Cave Hill: U.W.I., 1986).

—. *Traditional Folk Songs of Barbados*. (Bridgetown: MacMarson Associates, 1981).

Martin, Tony. *The Pan-African Connection*. (Dover: The Majority Press, 1983).

May, Chris. *African All-Stars: The Pop Music of A Continent*. (London: Quartet Books, 1987).

Meredith, Henry. *An Account of the Gold Coast of Africa*. (London: Frank Cass and Co Ltd., 1812).

Merriam, Alan. "The African Idiom in Music." *Journal of American Folklore*. 75 (1962) 120-130.

—. *The Anthropology of Music*. (Bloomington: Northwestern University Press, 1964).

Merwe, Peter. *Origins of the Popular Style: The Antecedents of Twentieth Century Popular Music*. (Oxford: Clarendon Press, 1989).

Middleton, Richard. *Studying Popular Music*. (Milton Keynes: Open University Press, 1990).

More than Drumming: Essays on African and Afro-Latin American Music and Musicians. Edited by Irene Jackson. (Connecticut: Greenwood Press, 1985).

Moreton, J.B. *Manners and Customs in the West India Islands*. (London, 1790).

Mukerfi, Chandra, et al. *Rethinking Popular Culture*. (Berkeley: University of California, 1991).

Murray, Albert. *Stomping The Blues*. (New York: McGraw-Hill Books Co., 1976).

Nettl, Bruno. *Theory and Method in Ethnomusicology*. (New York: Macmillan, 1964).

Nketia, J.H. Kwabena. "African Music and Western Praxis: A Review of Western Perspectives on African Musicology." *Canadian Journal of African Studies*. Vol. 20 No. 1 (1986) 36-56.

—. "Drum, Dance and Songs." *Atlantic Monthly*. (April 1959) 69-72.

—. *Folk Songs of Ghana*. (London: Oxford University Press, 1963).

—. *The Music of Africa*. (London: Victor Gollancz, 1975).

—. "The Musician in Akan Society." *The Traditional Artist in African Societies*. Edited by Warren L. D'Azvedo. 48-75.

—. "Traditional Music of the Ga People." *African Music*. Vol. 2 No. 1 (1958) 21-27.

—. "Unity and Diversity in African Music: A Pattern of Synthesis." Presented at the First Congress of Africanists (Accra, 1962).

Noel, Terry. *Pan Play*. (Stoke-on-Trent: Trentham Books, 1988).

Okpewho, Isidore. *African Oral Literature: Backgrounds, Character and Continuity*. (Bloomington: Indiana University Press, 1992).

—. "African Poetry: The Modern Writer and the Oral Tradition." *African Literature Today*. Edited by Eldred Jones. 1-24.

Oldmixon, J. *The British Empire in America Vol. 2*. (London, 1741).

Oral Poetry in Nigeria. Edited by Uchegbulam Abalogu. (Lagos: Nigeria Magazine, 1981).

Oral Traditional Literature. Edited by John Foley. (Ohio: Slavica Publications Inc., 1981).

Orderson, J. *Creoleana*. (London, 1842).

Parrish, Lydia. *Slave Songs of the Georgia Sea Islands*. (New York: Creative Age, 1942).

Parry, Milman. "The Studies in the Epic Techniques of Oral Verse Making I: Home and Homeric Style." *Harvard Studies in Classical Philosophy*. (1930) 73-135.

Pearse, Andrew. "Aspects of Change in Caribbean Folk Music." *Unesco International Folk Music Journal*. VII (1955) 29-36.

Peck, Philip. "The Power of Words in African Verbal Arts." *Journal of American Folklore*. Vol. 94 No. 371 (January-March 1981) 19-43.

Peck, Stephen. *Atlas of Facial Expression*. (New York: Oxford University Press, 1987).

The Performing Arts: Music and Dance. Edited by John Blacking. (New York: Mouton, 1979).

Perrone, Charles. *Masters of Contemporary Brazilian Song*. (Austin: University of Texas Press, 1989).

"The Persimmon Tree and the Beer Dance." Edited by William Smith. *Farmer's Register*. (April 6, 1839) 59-61.

Petrey, Sandy. *Speech Acts and Literary Theory*. (New York: Routledge, 1990).

Pidgin and Creole Linguistics. Edited by Albert Valdman. (Bloomington: Indiana University Press, 1977).

Pidginization and Creolization of Language. Edited by Dell Hymes. (Cambridge: Cambridge University Press, 1971).

Pinckard, G. *Notes on the West Indies Vol. 1*. (London, 1806).

Pitt, Harry. "Calypso from Patois to its Present Form." *Guardian Independence Supplement*. (August 26, 1962).

Pool, Rosey. *Beyond the Blues*. (Kent: Hand and Flower Press, 1962).

Popular Music and Communication. Edited by James Lull. (London: Sage Publications, 1987).

Purdie, Susan. *Comedy: the Mastery of Discourse*. (New York: Harvester Wheatsheaf, 1993).

Quevedo, Raymond. *Atilla's Kaiso: A Short History of the Trinidad Calypso*. (U.W.I: Extra-Mural Department, 1983).

Read, Alan. *Theatre and Everyday Life: An Ethics of Performance*. (London: Routledge, 1993).

Readings in Creole Studies. Edited by Ian Hancock. (Ghent: E. Story-Scienta PVBA, 1979).

Roberts, Peter. "Interpreting in a West Indian Language Situation." *Carib.* No. 3 (1983) 81-95.

—. "Linguistics and Language Learning." *Studies in Caribbean Languages.* Edited by Carrington. 230-244.

Rohlehr, Gordon. "Brathwaite with a Dash of Brown. Critic, the Writer and the Written Life." (St Augustine: U.W.I. 1988).

—. *Calypso and Society in Pre-Independence Trinidad.* (Tunapuna: H.E.M Printers Ltd., 1990).

—. "Masking in the Calypsos of Trinidad 1991." Paper at The Tenth Conference on West Indian Literature (St. Augustine: U.W.I., 1991).

—. *Pathfinder: Black Awakening in the Arrivants of E. K. Brathwaite.* (Tunapuna: The College Press, 1981).

—. "The Treatment of Women in Calypso." Twelve fifteen-minute programs (Trinidad: Government Broadcast Unit, 1975).

Romaine, Suzanne. *Pidgin and Creole Languages.* (London: Longman, 1988).

Roots and Branches: Current Directions in Slave Studies. Edited by Michael Craton. (Toronto: Penguin Press, 1977).

Rose, Andrew. *No Respect: Intellectuals and Popular Culture.* (New York: Routledge, 1989).

Roy, John. "The Structure of Tense and Aspect in Barbadian English Creole." *Focus on the Caribbean.* Edited by Manfred Gorlach. 141-156.

—. "Variation and Change in a Speech Community in Barbados." Ph.D. dissertation (Columbia University, 1984).

St. John, Bruce. *Bumbatuk: Poems in Barbadian Dialect.* (Bridgetown: Cedar Press, 1982).

Schechner, Richard. *Between Theatre and Anthropology.* (Philadelphia: University of Pennsylvania Press, 1985).

—. *Essays on Performance Theory 1970-1976.* (New York: Drama Book Specialists, 1977).

Schomburgk, Robert. *The History of Barbados.* (London: Frank Cass and Co. Ltd., 1848).

Schuller, Gunther. *Early Jazz: Its Roots and Musical Development.* (New York: Oxford University Press, 1968).

Searle, Chris. *Words Unchained: Language and Revolution in Grenada.* (London: Zed Books Ltd., 1984).

Sealey, John, et al. *Music in the Caribbean*. (London: Hodder and Stoughton, 1983).

Slavery, Colonialism and Racism. Edited by Sidney Mintz. (NewYork: W.W. Norton and Co Inc., 1974).

Sloan, Hans. *A Voyage to the Islands*. (London, 1707).

Sound Theory Sound Practice. Edited by Rick Altman. (NewYork: Routledge, 1992).

Source Materials for the Study of the Archeological and Pre-history of Barbados. Edited by Ronald Taylor. (St. Michael: Barbados Museum and Historical Society, 1991)

Speeches by Errol Barrow. Edited by Yussuff Haniff. (London: Hansib Publications, 1987).

Taylor, Douglas. *Languages of the West Indies*. (Baltimore: The Johns Hopkins University Press, 1977).

Thompson, Vincent Bakpetu. *The Making of the African Diaspora in the Americas 1441-1900*. (NewYork: Longman, 1986).

Tirro, Frank. *Jazz: A History*. (London: J.M. Dent and Sons Ltd., 1977).

Tonkin, Elizabeth. "Oracy and the disguises of Literacy." *Discourse and its Disguises*. Edited by Barber and Farias. 39-49.

Tornqvist, Egil. *Transposing Drama: Studies in Representation*. (Hampshire: McMillan, 1991).

Treves, Sir Frederick. *The Cradle of the Deep: An Account of a Voyage to the West Indies*. (London: Smith, Elden & Co., 1908).

Voiceprint. Edited by Gordon Rohlehr. (Essex: Longman, 1989).

Voices in Exile. Edited by Barbara Lalla. (Tuscaloosa: University of Alabama Press, 1989).

Wallis, Roger, et al. *Big Sounds from Small Peoples: The Music Industry in Small Countries*. (London: Constable and Co., 1984).

Ward, W.E.F. *A History of the Gold Coast*. (London: George Allen and Unwin Ltd., 1948).

Warner, Keith, Q. *The Trinidad Calypso: A Study of Calypso as Oral Literature*. (Washington: Three Continents Press, 1982).

Watts, David. *The West Indies: Patterns of Development, Culture and Environmental Change Since 1492*. (Cambridge: Cambridge University Press, 1987).

Weekes, Nathaniel. *Barbados.* (London: Privately printed, 1754).

Whiteley, Sheila. *The Space Between the Notes; Rock and the Counter-Culture.* (London: Routledge, 1992).

World Music, Politics and Social Change. Edited by Simon Frith. (Manchester: Manchester University Press, 1989).

Yankah, Kwesi. "The Making and Breaking of Kwame NKrumah: The Role of Oral Poetry." *Ghanaian Literatures.* Edited by Priebe. 45-55.

Yoruba Oral Tradition: Poetry in Music, Dance and Drama. Edited by Wande Abimbola. (Ibadan: Offset Lithography, 1975.)

Zaitsev, Igor, et al. *Soviet Rock: 25 Years in the Underground and Five Years of Freedom.* (Moscow: Progress Publishers, 1990).

Zumther, Paul. *Oral Poetry: an Introduction.* (Minneapolis: University of Minnesota Press, 1990).

ALSO OF INTEREST

Bob Marley
Davis, Stephen
330 pp., 1990, Revised Edition
Paper $18.95 (ISBN 0-87047-044-2)
A rebel, a visionary, an uncompromising champion of human rights—Robert
Nesta Marley rose from the slums of Kingston, Jamaica, to make reggae music
and his own message of rebellion, self-determination and the power of the
individual a spiritual and political force throughout the world. The Wailers
recording sessions, concerts and life at 56 Hope Road (Marley's residence) are
all part of this sensitive, authoritative and authentic look at the king of a musical
movement that swept out of Jamaica and into Western and Third World
countries alike. First published in 1985, this revised edition includes a post-
script describing Marley's continuing influence on the reggae scene.

Black Intellectuals and the Dilemmas of Race and Class in Trinidad
Oxaal, Ivar
334 pp., 1982
Paper $22.95 (ISBN 0-87073-417-2)
A perceptive description of the events leading to independence in the
multiracial setting of Trinidad. Covers the rise of Creole nationalism, the
role of intellectuals in Trinidad, and offers a social study of both Trinidad
and Tobago in the aftermath of independence.

Calamity in the Caribbean: Puerto Rico and the Bomb
Cripps, L.L.
185 pp., 1987
Paper $13.95 (ISBN 0-87047-035-3)
An incisive account of US plans to militarize Puerto Rico. Examines current political propaganda, the real and human costs of militarization, and what effect US policy will have on the Caribbean region.

Crime and Nation-Building in the Caribbean: The Legacy of Legal Barriers
Mahabir, Cynthia
280 pp., 1985
Cloth $24.95 (ISBN 0-87073-601-9)
Paper $18.95 (ISBN 0-87073-602-7)
Addresses the issue of Third World "lawbreakers" who press for freedom and equality with the ruling elites. Are they dangerous criminals or catalysts for necessary social change? Essential reading for sociologists, urban planners, criminologists, legislators and Caribbean and African-American history scholars.

Haiti's Bad Press
Lawless, Robert
Foreword by Jean Casimir, Haitian Ambassador to the US
228 pp., 1992
Cloth $25.95 (ISBN 0-87047-060-4)
Paper $14.95 (ISBN 0-87047-061-2)
Focusing on the long history of bias against Haiti and Haitians by foreign observers, Robert Lawless, an anthropologist, analyzes Haitian culture and politics from its eighteenth century origins to the present day, challenging "official" opinion. A source of accurate, sympathetic and culturally sensitive information, this book gives reasoned judgments, detailed information and impartial speculation about the future of Haiti and the US at a time when democracy is deeply threatened in Haiti and the rights of Haitians at home and abroad are in danger.

Black Dawn
Lloyd, Robin and Doreen Kraft
20 minutes, 1978
VHS video $29.95
Study guide $2.00
Animated paintings by thirteen of Haiti's foremost artists bring to life a Haitian folktale recounting the founding of the world's first independent Black republic. Winner of numerous awards, *Black Dawn* has captivated audiences around the world. Available in English, Creole or French.

Haitian Pilgrimage
Lloyd, Robin
27 minutes
VHS video $24.95
This video traces the journey of a Haitian-American family from Boston back to their roots in central Haiti. The family takes part in a Voodoo-Christian pilgrimage to the waterfall Saut D'Eau and the nearby church. The father, a sociology professor, is an initiated Voodoo priest. They discuss their heritage and make their journey home.

To order these titles or find out more about Schenkman Books, please contact us at:

Schenkman Books, Inc.
118 Main Street
Rochester, VT 05767 USA
(802) 767-3702 tel
(802) 767-9528 fax
schenkma@sover.net